Carlene & Michael Duffy

This Old Van

Plan, renovate and style your
own vintage caravan

Hardie Grant

EXPLORE

To our kids, Paddy and Stella, for being enthusiastic van-life memory-making participants and for bearing the brunt of what it takes for two parents to co-write a book. And to our family for picking up the slack when we were in the novel, all-consuming parallel universe that is book writing.

ABOUT THE AUTHORS

We are a husband-and-wife team who side-doored our way into the design and renovation space after our 2014 appearance on Australian renovation reality TV show *The Block*.

Michael is a qualified carpenter, licensed builder and now also a commercial pilot (he's busy), and Carlene owns and runs the Gold Coast–based interior design studio Cedar and Suede. We're parents to two funny, clever and strong-willed children, Paddy and Stella, and the most loved and loving, people-pleasing golden labrador, Harry.

We've been renovating for our entire married life, and since our TV experience we've wilfully immersed ourselves in every aspect of the home space, from designing and building to hosting design and renovation TV shows. But to this day, our most loved projects remain our five vintage vans.

Contents

A BIT ABOUT OUR VANS

There's something wistful and romantic about the idea of renovating a vintage caravan – maybe it's the freedom it alludes to. We'd love to tell you that we came up with the idea while lying on our backs on the grass, watching the clouds roll by and contemplating a future of long, winding roads and adventures, but the truth is disappointingly unromantic.

We grew up camping in tents on unpowered sites, with blow-up beds, cooler boxes that required a twice-a-day refill of ice, and no running water. We'd like to think that as adults we are still adventurous enough to enjoy this approach to camping, but we'd be fooling ourselves. We live busy lives, and holidaying in a tent the packing, set-up, pack down, and unpacking and everything in between – all felt like more work with only moments of down time.

A van was the solution. It allows us to have camping holidays without the discomfort that comes with scampering to keep the bedding away from the tent sides in torrential rain and without the disappointment of retrieving fruit and vegetables submerged in the melted ice at the bottom of the cooler box.

Why a vintage van and not a new van? It was plainly and simply the only thing we could afford. We are designers and renovators with creative, busy minds, and we get a buzz from big modification, so at the time, a vintage van felt accessible but also provided big transformative opportunities. So that's how it began. A very pragmatic thought became the most impactful and reverberating project we've ever done.

The interest in our vans was unexpected. We've connected with people from around the world who have been swept up in the idea of what a van can add to their lives and are in need of advice.

A van can be more than a holiday home on wheels, and for some the idea of renovating a van comes from a place of necessity. We've been sought out by people in situations ranging from a 75-year-old lady wanting to renovate a van to live in on her daughter's property to a 16-year-old boy desperate for a space away from his younger siblings, and a single mum who wanted to give her teenage child their own room in a house that felt like it was bursting at the seams.

We're yet to quit our jobs and travel the country, as seems to be the popular dream, but we cannot overstate the freedom a van has afforded us. We're able to venture on an embarrassing number of holidays without breaking the bank, and we're able to provide our kids with exactly the sort of vacation that we know will be etched deeply and lovingly in their memories: long, lazy beach sessions; choreographing dance routines; communal dinners and playing games with the other park kids, or 'parkies' as we affectionately call them, when the sun goes down. Caravan park holidays provide the sorts of no-fuss, low-key holidays that will play in our children's heads like movie scenes long into their futures.

millie BY

CEDAR + SUEDE

PART ONE

Meet the fleet

The things we've learned about renovating a vintage van we've learned from our five ladies: Millie, Vonnie, Dolly, Bumblebee and our latest van, Goldie. These old gals will feature heavily throughout the book, providing case studies about what to do and what not to do, so it's only right to give them an official introduction.

Meet Millie

Origin: 1950s
Length: 16ft (4.9m)
Width: 7.2ft (2.2m)
Internal footprint: 120sq ft (11.2m²)
Sleeps: 4
Make: Millard Florida
Purchased: 2016
Exterior colours: Navy and white
Interior colours: Navy, powder blue and white

Millie was our first baby, and like any good first-time parents, we learned what we should and shouldn't do with our subsequent babies. Before us, Millie only had one owner, and when we found her, she'd been sitting under a house for 20 years, barely used and in well-loved vintage condition. If you're going to buy a vintage van, you want to find one like Millie.

Millie was our test dummy and was subject to some of our van renovation ignorance. This old gal underwent a fairly significant overhaul (more than she needed in hindsight). We replaced the kitchen cabinets and built a new king-size bed with two bunk beds above. The dining area remained, and we resurfaced the table and added new upholstery. The wardrobe door front was replaced, she got a fresh coat of paint inside and out, and we installed new appliances.

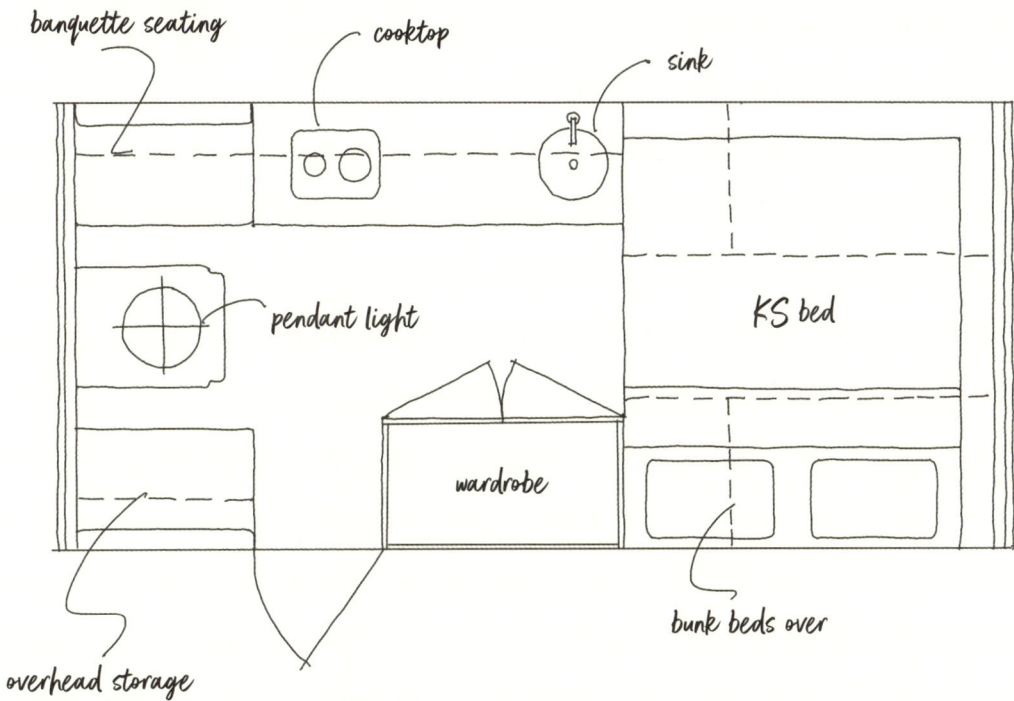

banquette seating

cooktop

sink

pendant light

KS bed

wardrobe

overhead storage

bunk beds over

Meet Vonnie

Origin: 1970s
Length: 15ft (4.6m)
Width: 7.5ft (2.3m)
Internal footprint: 112sq ft (10.4m^2)
Sleeps: 4
Make: Viscount
Purchased: 2017
Exterior colours: Spearmint green and white
Interior colours: Forest green, spearmint green and white

Vonnie was van number two, and with this '70s Viscount we were able to apply what we'd learned from renovating Millie. We renovated Vonnie as part of a paint-marketing campaign, so it was our opportunity to do a more superficial makeover and simply provide some resurfacing solutions, rather than carry out a substantial renovation.

All the cabinetry in Vonnie remained intact, and we revitalised it with fresh paint and new cabinet handles. We also preserved the original dining space and simply resurfaced what was there. Beyond that, we added new flooring, appliances, and curtains and utilised soft furnishings to bring new life to an old van. Vonnie was also the only van whose exterior we painted ourselves (all our other vans have been painted by an auto-painter), so she is by and large our most cost-effective transformation.

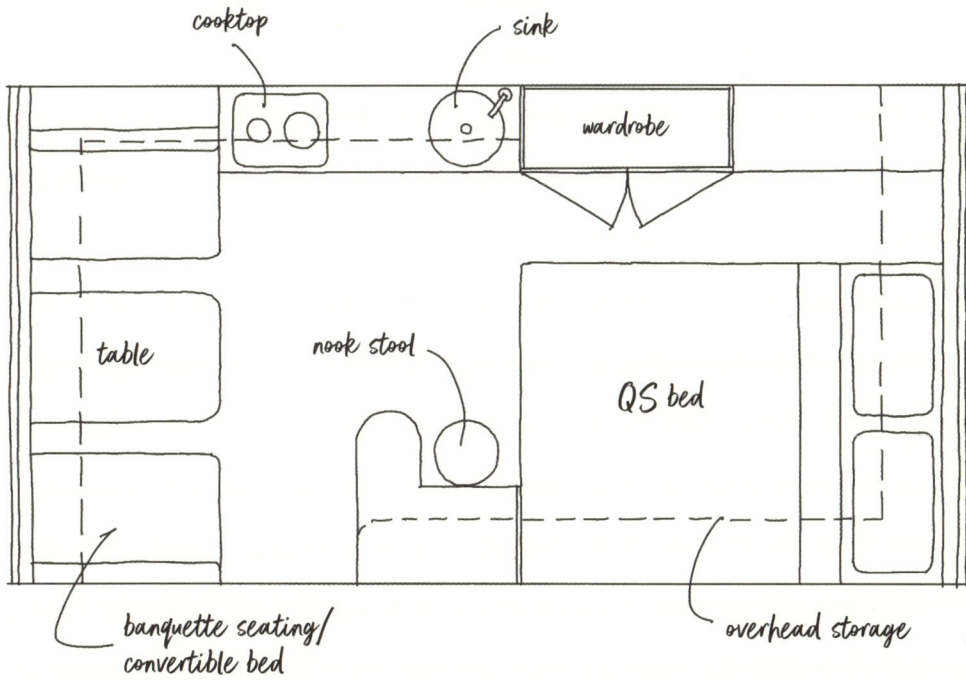

cooktop

sink

wardrobe

table

nook stool

QS bed

banquette seating/
convertible bed

overhead storage

Meet Dolly

Origin: 1970s
Length: 22ft (6.7m)
Width: 7.5ft (2.3m)
Internal footprint: 165sq ft (15.3m²)
Sleeps: 4
Make: Viscount
Purchased: 2017
Exterior colours: Powder blue and white
Interior colours: Powder blue, navy and white

This big, beautiful Viscount was named in honour of Dolly Everett, a 16-year-old who tragically took her life at the beginning of 2018 after enduring relentless cyber bullying. She left us with wise words beyond her years: 'Speak even if your voice shakes'. Dolly's favourite colour was blue and therefore so is our Dolly.

When we started renovating Dolly, we intended to finish the job and sell her, but Dolly's huge size made the idea of keeping her for our own family holidays very appealing, and she ended up being our wheels of choice for four very good years, before we sold her in 2022. This old gal served us well, and let's just say it was a bittersweet goodbye.

Like Vonnie, Dolly had a lot of cabinetry in good condition that we could retain and simply rejuvenate. Once again, we were able to paint it and use it largely as it was, just adding new brass mesh inserts on the kitchen fronts. We cut the too large dining booth down in size to allow for bunk beds and included new kitchen appliances, new flooring and new bench and table surfaces. Dolly boasted a huge amount of bench space for a van, a luxury which we agreed to not get used to, as we'll likely never have so much space again.

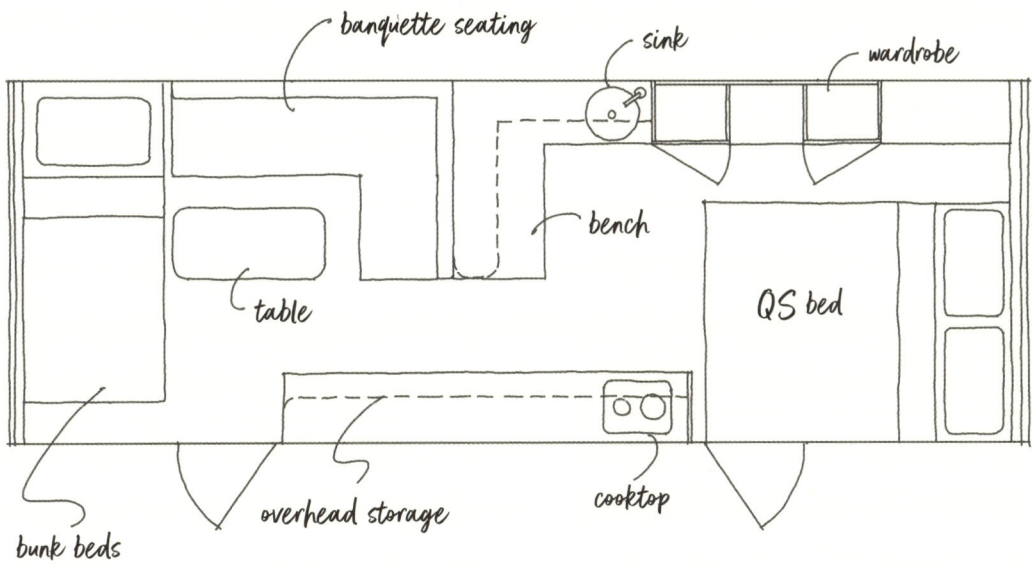

banquette seating

sink

wardrobe

bench

table

QS bed

bunk beds

overhead storage

cooktop

Meet Bumblebee
aka BB

Origin: 1970s
Length: 12ft (3.7m)
Width: 7.2ft (2.2m)
Internal footprint: 90sq ft (8.4m^2)
Sleeps: 2–4
Make: Franklin
Purchased: 2018
Exterior and interior colours: Yellow and white

Our smallest but arguably most popular transformation, Bumblebee, takes her name from the Transformers, because well, we transformed her, and Carlene really wanted to do a yellow van, so it all just worked towards her cause. At only 12ft (3.7m) long, BB was the first van we renovated that was more tailored to a couple than a family, and it was also the first and only van we renovated specifically for resale. From that one experience,

we learned that while you may make some money from flipping caravans, you'd need to find a way of streamlining the process to make it worthwhile – which isn't that simple when dealing with all the quirks that come with a vintage van.

In BB, we demolished only what we had to. We got rid of two single beds to make way for one double bed. The dining area was simply resurfaced with a new laminate tabletop and new upholstery for the bench seats. The framework of the original wardrobe remained but we added new door fronts. The lower cabinets of the kitchen were replaced with new cabinets; however, the original upper cabinets were kept and simply received new fronts. Fresh paint inside and out, together with new lighting and soft furnishings, was enough to bring this little lady back to life.

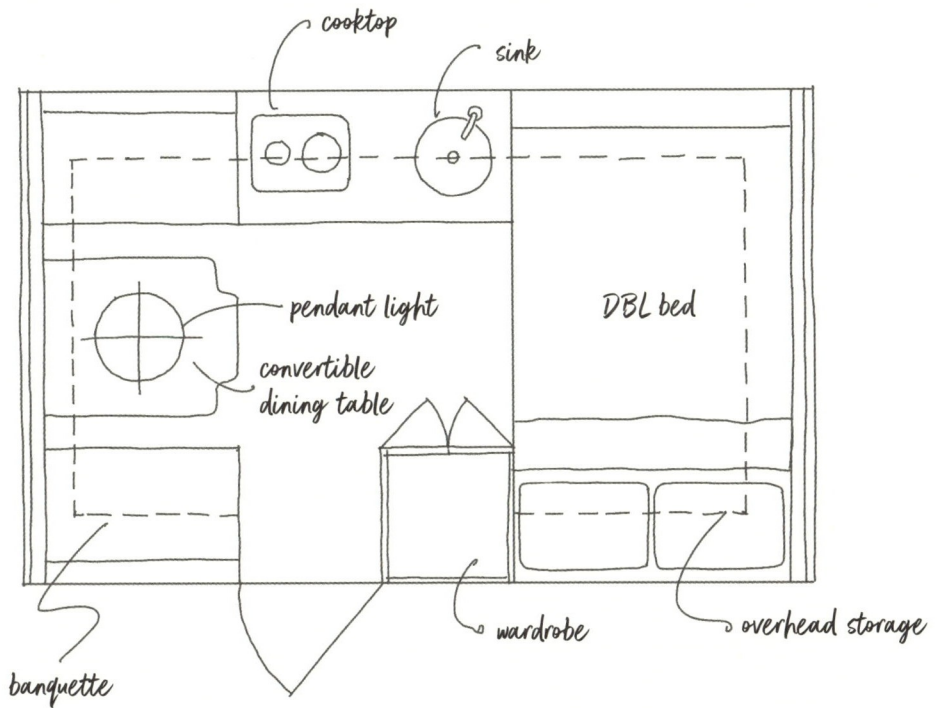

cooktop

sink

pendant light

DBL bed

convertible
dining table

banquette

wardrobe

overhead storage

Meet Goldie

Origin: 1970s
Length: 18ft (5.5m)
Width: 7.5ft (2.3m)
Internal footprint: 135sq ft (12.5m²)
Sleeps: 4 (5 if you include the built-in sofa)
Make: Viscount
Purchased: 2017
Exterior and interior colours: Sunset colours (such as dusky pinks, plum, peachy) medium coloured timber)

Our most recent vintage belle is named in honour of our hometown of the Gold Coast, and her colour scheme pays tribute to golden hour, our favourite time of day. We purchased Goldie around the same time we found Dolly, back in 2017, and until recently she'd been sitting under our house waiting patiently for her moment in the sun.

There was nothing to retain in this van, so we had little choice but to take her back to her shell and start from scratch. We used the opportunity to come up with a layout that worked for us and our two tween kids. After a few years of vanning experience and a more comprehensive understanding of what worked and didn't work for us in our previous vans, Goldie was our opportunity to create something just right for us. We prioritised comfortable sleeping conditions (beds and window dressings) and sufficient, accessible storage space. Apart from the vintage wardrobe, Michael built every piece of joinery from scratch in this van. For the first time, we installed carpet as our flooring of choice – we know what you're thinking, but bear with us and keep reading to understand why it makes sense. Goldie is not one for 'the people'; she's for us – but we think you'll love her nonetheless.

banquette seat

fold down bunks

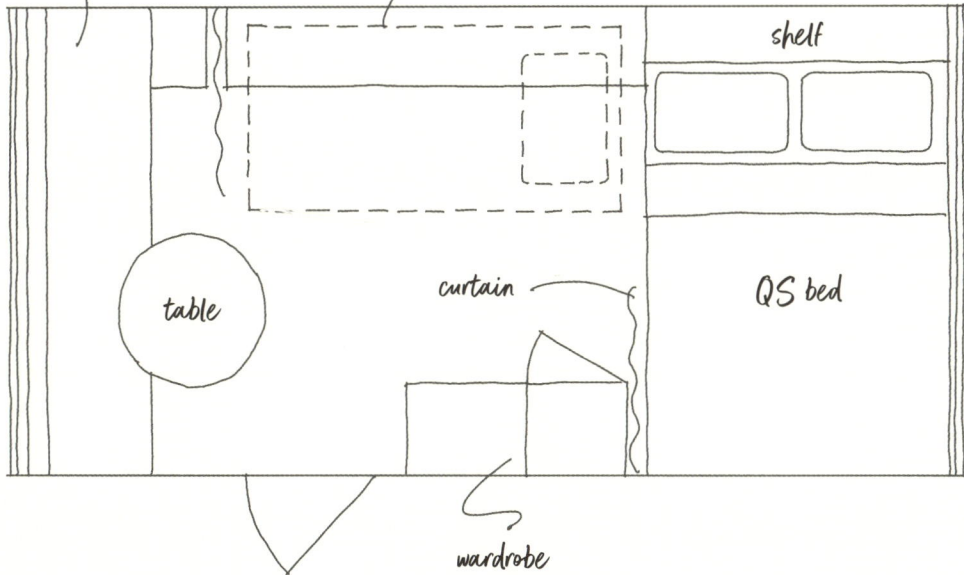

shelf

table

curtain

QS bed

wardrobe

PART TWO

Buying a vintage van

What you look for in a van is going to be very personal to your specific situation, including your budget, skill set and location, to name a few. But there are some overall things to look out for to ensure you wind up with a van that suits your needs and doesn't end up revealing more problems than it's worth.

THINGS TO CONSIDER
BEFORE YOU START LOOKING

Think of who you're accommodating and your skill set when looking for a van.

WHO ARE YOU ACCOMMODATING?

The number of people you need to accommodate should be your first consideration when looking for a vintage van to purchase. Ask yourself these questions before you even start your search:

- How many beds do you require?

- What size beds do you need?

- Are you comfortable with the idea of converting the dining table to a bed every night and back to a dining table in the morning?

- Are you going to attach an annex that can also house beds?

WHAT'S YOUR SKILL SET?

Your skill set will come into play thereafter. The second-hand van market is diverse, and there is everything out there from full strip-outs to vans that have been half renovated before a weary renovator has thrown in the towel. Are you a jack-of-all-trades with the time and skills to tackle a substantial renovation, or do you have the budget to outsource the entire project to professionals? You might lie somewhere in between. Where you sit on this spectrum is going to weigh heavily in the decision process of the type of van you are going to purchase.

SHAPE AND TYPE OF VAN

The shape of the van is wildly important, because unless you plan on making significant structural changes (we don't) then there's not much you can do to alter the shape through a renovation.

The ideal van shape obviously comes down to personal opinion, so the best way to decide what you like and don't like is to do your research. There is so much inspiration on Pinterest and Instagram, and you will easily be able to refine your search parameters to pinpoint what is right for you. There are some beautiful old vans out there, but there are also plenty of 'stinkers', so remember that just because the ad says it's vintage, it doesn't always mean that the ugly duckling will turn into a swan.

Personally, we love the shape of the old Viscounts. They are wide with a visually aesthetic facade, and the corner windows offer a great aspect from inside the van and let in much-enjoyed light.

CONVENTIONAL VAN

Conventional vans have a full-height roof and solid walls. They don't require any set-up or pack down and are always accessible when travelling on the road. They offer plenty of storage options and are consistently our pick when looking for vans to purchase.

WIND-UP VAN

A wind-up van's walls are made up of solid panelling on the lower half and canvas on the upper half. Because they are compact when packed away, they are a good option if they are to be stored in a residential garage; however, once you arrive at your destination, these vans require considerable set-up. They are inaccessible until they are set up, they offer no up-high storage options, and the wind-up mechanism can become a maintenance issue.

POP-TOP VANS

A pop-top van is a combination of a conventional caravan and a wind-up camper van. Offering the benefits of a full-height van once set up, a pop-top van packs away for improved aerodynamics while towing and a lower height for storing. This van still requires set-up on arrival; however, the inside can always be accessed and the extensions provide extra sleeping space.

Airstreams

The Airstream is an iconic American towable van with a notable, bullet-like frame and polished aluminium coachwork, and renovating one has long been on Michael's bucket list.

This highly coveted van has been in production since the 1930s, and many vintage models are still made today, with a few models designed specifically for Europe and its narrow roads.

Nearly 30 different models of Airstreams have been produced over the decades, and each era has influenced the model's unique shape.

Airstreams are typically larger than most Australian vans and are also substantially more kitted-out, generally always including bathrooms and bedrooms. The cost of an Airstream, even one that has not been renovated, also far exceeds the cost of any vintage Australian model.

Chloe McConchie is the owner of Aluminia, which imports Airstreams from the United States for sale in Australia. She says the cost of an Airstream varies according to the model, era, condition, level of restoration, size and location.

Furthermore, when buying them outside of the United States, international shipping costs and import taxes have to be factored into their sale price, undoubtedly making them a luxury model.

Even in the United States, though, the prices are far beyond those of their Australian counterparts, and it's not unusual for a renovation or restoration to come in at significantly more than most people are willing to spend on any caravan, let alone a 50-year-old one.

When sourcing an Airstream, Chloe suggests that while all vintage Airstreams will have scratches and dents from life on the road, securing something with minimal damage is important. The structural condition of the van is also very important, so make sure to inspect the chassis, subfloor, windows and door, as well as the condition of the hardware.

The interior finishes of a vintage Airstream are also reminiscent of the era it was built. Airstreams from the 1950s and 1960s reflect a quintessential mid-century aesthetic, with timber joinery, bold-coloured appliances, patterned benchtops and graphic upholstery.

Airstreams from the 1970s don laminate cabinetry, those classic '70s hues of brown, green and orange, and floral wallpaper.

There are typically two types of Airstream renovators: those who value a genuine interior and work towards restoring the van to its original condition, paying homage to when it was build; and those who prefer a modern approach, favouring light timbers, neutral hues and contemporary fittings and fixtures.

Sheena and Jason Armstrong fall into the latter camp. Residing in Atlanta, Georgia, these keen vanners bought and renovated a 31ft (9.5m) 1977 Airstream Sovereign to fulfil an idyllic dream life on the road. Meet Mavis, or Mavis 2.0, in fact. Like Millie did for us, Mavis 1.0 provided Sheena and Jason with a plethora of lessons they could apply to Mavis 2.0.

This duo knew from the moment they decided to purchase a van that it had to be an Airstream. To Sheena and Jason this iconic van is like rolling art, but getting the old van to this point took some work. It took two years of hard work to just get Mavis ready for the rebuild. They took her all the way down to the frame, and with 40 years of life under its belt the trailer needed significant repairs and reinforcement. With everything down to a shell, they also took the opportunity to completely redo the insulation and electrical wiring, and they installed a new subfloor.

Sheena's dad, who runs the van remodelling business NuAbode, assisted with the renovation and equates working on an Airstream to building inside a fishbowl: 'Nothing is square, nothing is even, nothing is flat'.

In planning their renovation, Sheena and Jason had a few requirements to make the van work for them functionally while on the road. Because they planned to work while they travelled, two workspaces with a dividing door were a non-negotiable. Another imperative for the couple was a king-size bed, and consequently the bed in Mavis spans their van bedroom from wall to wall; the couple love the feeling of cosiness it creates. An on-demand hot-water system was another luxury the couple were sure they wanted to include. Sheena thinks there's nothing better than knowing you can come back to a hot shower after a full day exploring.

The couple travelled full-time in their Airstream for almost two years, making their way across the country and back, twice. They say they had enough experiences to reminisce over for a lifetime and lapped up the pleasure of the ever-changing landscapes. When they grew tired of one spot, they would just hitch up and move on.

Sheena and Jason refer to it as the ultimate freedom, but there's no place like home and, eventually, they reached a point where they missed their family and friends enough to return to their hometown and put down roots. The couple still enjoy trips in Mavis, but these days their trips are short and sweet.

TOWING ABILITY AND CAPACITY

If you are a vanning novice, this may not be the time to seek out a 31ft (9.5m) Airstream. Towing a van can take some getting used to, and the bigger the van the more challenging it will be to handle on the road. If you've ever watched anyone try to steer a caravan into the increasingly tight spaces provided by caravan park sites, you'll know that starting small is key. We suggest beginning with a 16–18ft (4.9–5.5m) van for a family or a 12ft (3.7m) van for a couple, and working your way up if you want to. It's also worth pointing out to van-towing rookies that there are towing-education services out there – simply punch it into your search engine to find one in your area. It's certain to make you more comfortable on the road, as well as keep you, your family and other motorists safe.

Knowing your vehicle's towing capacity is extremely important when choosing which type of van to purchase. Buying a van that is too heavy for your vehicle is not only counter to regulations but is also dangerous. A van that's too heavy can make your trailer swing, causing you to lose control of your vehicle, and can create difficulties in stopping. When you get a tow bar installed, the supplier will add a plate on the inside of the driver's side door that will indicate your tow bar rating. Generally, you should aim to have about 150–300kg (330–660lb) on the tow ball.

To determine your vehicle's towing capacity, you'll first need to understand some specific terms:

THE VEHICLE

Kerb weight: The total weight of your vehicle with only the driver and liquids, such as oil and fuel.

Tow ball weight: The amount of weight exerted by the van on your vehicle's tow ball. You can check this weight by using a tow ball weight scale. For safety, this generally needs to be less than 10 per cent of the total load; otherwise, it takes the weight off the front wheels of the car, which can make directional control difficult.

Vehicle payload: The weight of anything you add to your vehicle, including gear, cargo and passengers. This also includes the weight exerted by the van on your vehicle's tow ball.

THE TRAILER

Tare mass: The weight of your van, including accessories but not cargo.

Trailer payload: The weight of anything additional you add to your van, including cargo.

Aggregate trailer mass (ATM): The total mass of the van when carrying the maximum load recommended by the manufacturer.

Gross trailer mass (GTM): The weight of your van when attached to your vehicle.

THE LIMITS

Aggregate weight rating: The maximum allowed weight of your van, including all gear and cargo. The tare mass + trailer payload can't exceed this amount.

Gross combined weight rating: The maximum amount your vehicle and van can safely weigh when loaded. Your kerb weight + vehicle payload + tare mass + trailer payload cannot exceed this amount.

These limits will be stated on the vehicle's VIN (Vehicle Identification Number) plate, usually found on a sticker on the driver's side door or in the owner's manual. Take time to calculate the weights correctly.

Start by researching the market to gain
an understanding of what's out there.

WHERE TO SOURCE

Start by researching the market to gain an understanding of what's out there, the range of brands, asking prices and the variance in conditions. This will stand you in good stead when it's time to negotiate with your seller.

We've sourced all of our vans online from Gumtree, but we also recommend scouring websites like Craigslist, Caravan Camping Sales, Facebook Marketplace and eBay. In fact, a simple Google search will provide you with a huge range of options from various sellers.

On top of some late-night scrolling, start telling everyone you know that you're in the market for a vintage van. We've had multiple people contact us over the years to let us know they had vans on their property that they'd love for someone to come and take off their hands.

PURCHASE PRICE

We've purchased vans ranging in price from AU$500 to AU$6000 (US$370–US$4500/£280–£3400), depending on their condition. That said, we haven't purchased a van since 2017, and the second-hand van market has recently seen a huge surge in prices.

When vintage van renovating really started gaining momentum a few years ago, so did their prices. Owners quickly realised the value of the piece of metal sitting in their backyard, and the pandemic has further added to the inflation.

Since the recent pandemic drove prices and demand for caravans up, you'd be unlikely to find an unrenovated vintage van for AU$500 these days, with prices typically upwards of AU$3000 (US$2000/£1675) for something towable.

THINGS TO CONSIDER BEFORE YOU BUY

The importance of a pre-purchase inspection cannot be overstated. Michael was lax with the inspection for Bumblebee, having already decided to buy the van simply based on the photo alone and irrespective of its condition. Let's just say the impulsive approach is flawed. He returned home with a van that turned out to have a timber frame. 'No problem. I'm a carpenter. How bad can it be?' The answer is: very bad! It required a significant rebuild, to the point where Michael reconstructed almost 60 per cent of the van's entire frame. Had he been vigilant with the pre-purchase inspection, he would have seen the warning signs that lay beneath the perfectly shaped exterior.

WATER DAMAGE

When inspecting the van, decide whether you will do a complete strip-out, partially demolish it or leave the interior intact. Water damage to materials you will replace is not a deal-breaker, but if you decide you merely want to make simple cosmetic changes, and you won't be replacing the materials, then checking for water damage is crucial. Water damage typically presents in the swelling of timber cabinetry and water stains around windows, skylights, roof hatches and vents. Another indicator of potential water damage is if the van shows heavy use of silicon on the exterior, which is often a sign that the previous owner has attempted to stop leaks.

RUST

Check the chassis for any obvious signs of rust. The most common place for rust to be present is around the hitch and drawbar. The chassis will almost always have surface rust, which can be easily treated with rust-inhibiting paint (see page 165). However, rust that is starting to bubble through paintwork or has completely eaten a hole through the chassis is a potential red flag and should prompt further investigation, although it isn't necessarily a deal-breaker. If there are only rust spots here and there, then it may be an easy fix for a welder. If the chassis is riddled with rust, it's your cue to walk away and look for another option.

The importance of a pre-purchase inspection cannot be overstated.

WINDOWS

Be sure to check that all existing window frames are intact. It is common for owners to pull out windows to install the old 'window rattler' air conditioner. This can pose a potential problem, because vintage van window frames can be hard, if not impossible, to source. On the other hand, the glass is easily replaced, and a lot of owners opt to replace the glass with acrylic of the same thickness. Many suppliers will cut to size if you can provide them with a template. Window stays and locks are readily available online, and my bet is that most of your van's will need restoring or replacing.

VAN CLADDING

Depending on your plans for the exterior, the cladding can make or break your project. You will be very lucky to find a 50-year-old van that doesn't have a mark on it; however, too many holes, dents, bumps and scrapes will mean a lot of work down the track and may not be worth the time or cost of fixing them. Some caravan profiles have been discontinued, meaning you will be unable to buy replacement panels.

MECHANICS

During the pre-purchase inspection, Michael always checks to ensure that the van is, at a minimum, safe to tow home. Inspect wheels, brakes, bearings and the hitch, and ensure there are no loose items that might blow off. Check the requirements for towing unregistered vehicles in your state or country with local transportation authorities, as the regulations can differ significantly. If the van does not have working lights, a trailer lightboard can be attached.

BRAKES

Check with your local governing body for brake requirements specific to your area. Use the following as a general guide:

Australian regulations

- Vans up to 750kg (1650lb) do not require brakes.

- Vans over 750kg (1650lb) require mechanical brakes.

- Vans over 2t (4400lb) require electric brakes and a breakaway that applies the van's brakes if the van becomes detached from the vehicle.

United Kingdom regulations

- Vans up to 750kg (1650lb) do not require brakes but should not weigh more than 50 per cent of your vehicle weight.

- Vans over 750kg (1650lb) must use a breakaway cable or secondary coupling in case the trailer becomes detached from your car. The car and loaded van must not weigh over the second weight shown on the car manufacturer's plates (for more information see page 27).

United States regulations

- Each state has its own regulations for the types of brakes required for each van size. The regulations need to be observed not only where the van is registered but also in the states in which you'll be travelling.

PART THREE

Design & planning

The design phase is key to ensuring your renovation or restoration runs as smoothly and efficiently as possible. We've been known to get excited, jump the gun and start demolition and construction before we were completely ready, so trust us when we say the more time you spend in the design phase, the more equipped you'll be to face the little surprises that will almost certainly present along the way.

BUDGETING

The million-dollar question! How much do you need to budget for your van renovation? Well, how long is a piece of string? It's nearly impossible to give advice on van renovation costs due to all the variables that come with each unique brand of van, its condition and your own personal skill set.

Research, meticulous planning and careful selection of the van and materials can save you a lot of money, and so can doing the work yourself; however, the costs of materials and tools add up too, so make sure you factor that in.

It's a good idea to create a detailed budget for your renovation and then add 20–25% extra for unforeseen expenses – things always end up being more expensive than you think. Update the budget with the actual costs throughout the process to make sure you stay on track.

BUILDING YOUR DESIGN CONCEPT

RESEARCH, RESEARCH, RESEARCH

When we renovated our first van, Millie, there was next to no material out there from which to seek inspiration. That's no longer the case. A simple Google or Pinterest search will generate plenty of renovated vintage vans, but in order to ensure our vans don't all start looking alike, we strongly recommend seeking inspiration beyond other vintage vans. Home interiors and commercial spaces provide oodles of visual stimuli, but Carlene has been known to find inspiration in fashion, nature, art and even vintage cars and boats.

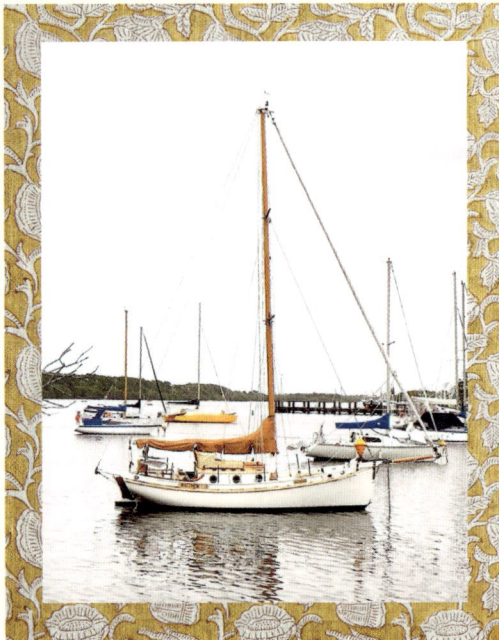

This sweet sailing boat that Carlene ogles every year during our annual holiday influenced Bumblebee's outcome.

Think of white, black, timber and metals as colours too, and restrict your colour palette to a just few different colours.

COLOUR PALETTE

Start by deciding your colour palette. Simply locking this in will help guide all your other choices. It creates parameters, and in a world of infinite options, parameters will be your friend.

In general, Carlene's approach to colour has always been about saturating a space to create tonality, rather than applying lots of different colours, which creates high contrast. High contrast can feel chaotic, which isn't how she wants her space to feel – especially not a small space like a van.

By layering one colour in different shades, she's able to create a feeling of calm and sophistication, and, more importantly, a space we won't tire of. We know what works for us, but you need to work out what works for you. Think of white, black, timber and metals as colours too, and restrict your colour palette to a just few different colours, which can then be used in different shades and tones.

When building your colour palette, timber and metal should be considered in context to your overall scheme and the feel you want to achieve.

STEP OUTSIDE YOUR COMFORT ZONE

Your van most likely isn't your permanent home. Rather, it's probably your holiday home, so why not renovate it to be a refreshing departure from the surroundings you're accustomed to? If there was ever a time to follow through with something you've been too nervous to try in your own home, this is it.

More than that, these vans are vintage vans. The '50s, '60s, '70s and even '80s were times of confident choices, vibrant colours and dynamic patterns. While Carlene doesn't advocate applying psychedelic colours to a van designed for modern living, she wholeheartedly condones paying homage to the era through the use of saturated colour.

Using colour can be a scary concept for many, although Carlene's inclined to think the hesitancy is less in deciding on a general colour and more in being able to apply it to a scheme. Let's do this one step at a time.

CREATE AN INSPIRATION BOARD

Once you have a general colour palette in mind, use Pinterest to start pinning anything and everything you like within that colour scheme. It can be anything from fashion to nature to art. This visual reference will help keep you on track – keep it close and keep coming back to it as a visual guide. This first step does not need to be representative of products you would ultimately use in your van but is simply about being inspired and seeing it develop into a loose concept.

The inspiration boards here and on the previous pages reflect Carlene's first step in pulling together a scheme. Not all of these materials will end up in the final product, but it is enough to get the creative juices flowing and provide confidence in what you're doing.

CREATE A MATERIALS BOARD

Once you have your inspiration board and you're happy with what you're seeing, you can then take the next step and create a board consisting exclusively of the actual products to be included in your van.

Canva is an online graphic design platform created for the layperson, and we've found it to be an excellent tool for pulling together materials boards. It's incredibly user-friendly, and it allows you to see all of your selections in one place. It provides templates that allow you to simply replace their image with yours. It's also completely fine to simply copy and paste images into a Word document if you'd rather. Remember, this is for your benefit only.

These material boards were created with Canva using materials suitable for a van.

Aged brass cabinet knobs

Oversized woven pendant

Rattan mesh cabinet front inserts

Light oak timber cabinet frames

In Millie, rather than paint the interior navy like the exterior, Carlene selected a powder blue and referenced the navy exterior by painting the beds navy and incorporating navy accents through the soft furnishings, such as the bench seat upholstery.

Oversized rattan pendant

Penny round mosaic tile used for dining table surface

Timber-look vinyl plank flooring

Brass shell pull handle for cabinets

In Vonnie and Dolly, Carlene selected the exterior paint colours and simply mirrored them inside. Once inside, deciding what colours go on what surfaces could potentially be workshopped on the go, but know that minimising high contrast will help in keeping your space feel calm and cohesive.

In Vonnie, all our cabinetry was painted spearmint green and all walls and the ceiling were painted white (see pages 51 and 57).

Spearmint paint colour

Subway-look Tic Tac tiles

Forest green upholstery

Timber-look vinyl plank flooring used on the floor and on some benches

In Dolly, we went further with the colour and painted all the surfaces inside powder blue apart from the overhead cabinets and ceiling. In original vintage vans, the cabinet fronts are often painted a contrasting colour to the cabinet base, or have a timber grain laminate front on a white base. This may upset the van traditionalists, but Carlene strongly discourages the two-tone approach to van cabinets. Painting the front a contrasting colour to the cabinet base makes the fronts appear itty-bitty and creates visual busyness, something you want to avoid in small spaces.

If your digital material board isn't enough, you could take it one step further and order physical samples of your desired products to create a materials board.

Palm pattern upholstery

Brash mesh used for cabinet fronts

Original cabinet knobs

Benches made from laminate sheet on board

DECIDING ON THE PAINT COLOURS

When building your materials board, there is no right place to start, but Carlene likes to begin with paint colours – specifically, the exterior paint colour. It's the simplest place to start because here you're not contending with multiple surfaces but rather just one large surface.

In our first four vans, we always selected a colour for the bottom half of the van and a white for the top half. After the success of Millie, it felt like a tried and tested, ol' faithful approach that we knew worked. White is a colour too and can vary significantly in the undertone. It can in fact pull significant focus, so use it in a considered way instead of as a default choice. For more information about whites and how to create a neutral colour scheme see pages 70–1.

White is a colour too and can in fact pull significant focus, so use it in a considered way instead of as a default choice.

Contrasting fabric patterns

Brass wall lamps

Low-pile carpet tiles

Sheer linen curtains

Before hitting go on your design, give yourself permission to add and delete again and again until you feel comfortable with your combination of choices.

In the case of Goldie, Carlene was very tempted to break the pattern and try two saturated colours on the exterior separated vertically rather than horizontally. When it came to painting day, however, she had a change of heart. Because vans are always longer than they are high, it made the most sense to carve up the colour horizontally as we'd always done. In an effort to make Goldie live up to her name and reflect golden hour, Carlene's paint colours needed to evoke mood and atmosphere. The peachy pink and dark berry colour on the facade are carried through inside with the introduction of dusky pinks, honey and mustard colours in the interiors.

To feel fully encompassed by colour it was important in this scheme that no white appear anywhere. It can be easy to think that a neutral like white won't pull focus, but the opposite is true. White can in fact very much command a space, so it needs to be well considered just like any other colour.

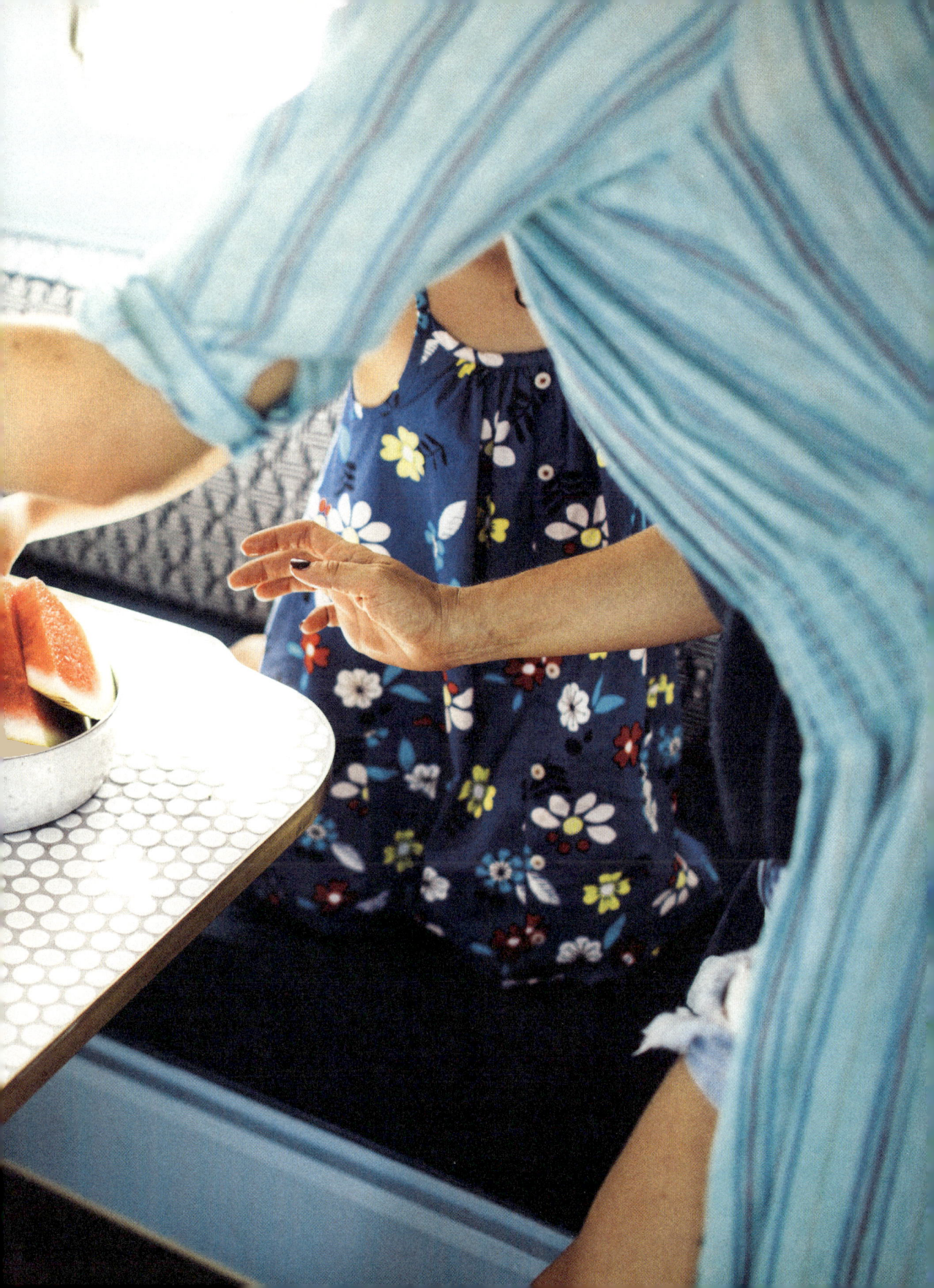

Make sure you observe the colour after two coats of thoroughly dried paint and study it at different times of the day to see how the colour interacts with the changing light.

SAMPLE, SAMPLE, SAMPLE

Sampling your paint colours in situ is key to ensuring you're getting the colour you want. No number of paint sample tins is too many, and sampling your paint in large swatches on the actual material is key. Colours can appear different based on the surface they appear on. Colours will also vary depending on the quality of natural light the space receives. For example, on the exterior cladding, the colours will look lighter when the sunlight is directly hitting it as opposed to when it's in the shade, where the colours will appear darker and more saturated. Similarly, the colour you've sampled on the exterior cladding can look different on the interior surfaces.

Sampling is the only way to get your colours right. Don't settle for close enough. This part of the design process is key to its success.

CHOOSING MATERIALS

In Bumblebee the light oak materials are the hero. Applying timber on the joinery fronts meant it accounts for most of the vertical surfaces and in a small space – like little 11 ft (3.5m) Bumblebee – it acts as the dominant colour.

TIMBER

Consider timber in terms of your overall colour scheme. Like paint colours, timber comes in a huge range of shades, from bleached white all the way to very dark brown, depending on the timber type and your stain of choice.

In the cases of Millie, Vonnie, Dolly and Bumblebee, wherever we employed timber, or any timber-look materials like the flooring, we did so in light to medium timber tones. For example, Dolly's bunk ladder and Bumblebee's kitchen are both constructed in light-coloured oak, and it feels fresh and coastal amidst the tones of the paint colours we selected. In Millie, Dolly and Vonnie, timber was used in fairly small doses and provides more of an accent colour/material. In fact, our only use of timber in Vonnie was where we used a timber-look vinyl plank on the floor and as the nook countertop. On the flip side, in Bumblebee and Goldie we used timber in a much more substantial way, in a manner that meant it dictated the overall scheme.

When building your colour pallette consider timber a colour. The above is a small sample of different coloured stains applied to an oak timber. It's an indicator of just how significant a timber colour can be within your interior scheme.

In Goldie we opted to invest in the moodiness of the interior scheme by utilising a darker timber, paying homage to its retro roots. The darker colour is also effective at creating a backdrop from which the other colours can shine.

Michael used bracing plywood for all internal cladding in Goldie, which we found to be a cost-effective, lightweight and effective cladding solution. We love the colour in the context of the paint and fabric colours we opted for in this scheme. It brings warmth and is a definitive nod to the '70s aesthetic we were adamant to celebrate.

Matt black

Aged nickel

Stainless steel

Polished nickel

Polished chrome

Matt white

Living copper

Living bronze

Brushed copper

Brushed rose gold

polished rose gold

Polished brass

Brushed brass

Metals are colours too. Whether you choose bronze, brass, copper, black, gunmetal grey or chrome, the colour should be considered in the context of your colour scheme.

METALS

If you choose to incorporate a living (or organic) metal in your van, you need to be prepared for it to patinate over time. This means the surface will change with time and use and will be subject to watermarking and oxidisation due to handling, cleaning and climatic changes. We love a living metal and the way it changes and darkens over time, but if you don't like surprises and prefer the finish of your metals to appear clean and even, it's safer to stick with stainless steel or plated metals when it comes to things like tapware and handles.

Heavy use of shiny new metals has the risk of cheapening your interior, whereas aged brass and aged bronze (even the ones that are plated) tend to add a sense of old-world charm and sophistication that is impossible not to love.

Brass has long been Carlene's metal of choice in interior spaces, so naturally it also flowed through to our vans. She feels comfortable combining living brass – like the table edging we used in multiple vans and which will patinate over time – with brass-look products achieved by spray painting existing metal. She also thinks it's completely acceptable to add plated metals into the mix, like in the form of handles and hooks, and to mix new brass with aged brass. Plated metal is a thin layer of metal applied as a covering to the surface of an object.

Wall light and bench trim: living brass that will patinate over time

Shelf rail and stool legs: existing metal spray painted in gold for a brass look.

Cabinet knobs: superficially aged for a brass look

Patina is a chemical process that occurs on living metals due to exposure, climatic changes and use.

Mixing metals, such as chrome and black or chrome and brass, is also completely fine, but in a small space like a van, Carlene suggests limiting different coloured metals to no more than two, and she would avoid mixing metal colours for the same type of items. For example, if you choose black handles or knobs for your cabinets, use black for handles and knobs throughout the van. Then you can introduce another metal via something like wall hooks or the kitchen tap if you decide you want to mix metal colours. She also suggests keeping your handles and hinges within the same colour where you can.

Carlene has a personal dislike of mixing copper and brass, because they can be quite attention grabbing in their own right and are inclined to compete for attention, but context is everything and there are exceptions to every rule.

Carlene suggests limiting different metals to no more than two, and she would avoid mixing metal colours for the same type of items.

FABRICS

The power of fabric colours cannot be underestimated: in the case of a small space like a van, fabric choices can set the tone for your entire scheme. The role of fabrics is especially important in terms of the built-in upholstery, which is a fixed piece of furniture and therefore a semi-permanent decision.

Because we didn't reference the exterior yellow in the wall or joinery colours in Bumblebee's interior, the fabric had a big job to do. It needed to bring in the yellow but without being loud, like the vintage-look upholstery.

Carlene balanced out the colour by also referencing the yellow in the bedding. She used the same colour in both the quilt cover and pillowcases but in contrasting patterns – this is how she achieved tonality while creating interest. Be prepared to shop widely to get what you want – the pillowcases and the quilt cover in Bumblebee came from different retailers.

In Bumblebee, Carlene used two upholstery fabrics from the same range and with the same base cloth – which you could describe as beige or is often described as a 'linen' colour. It's essentially just the pattern that varies, which she loves. In addition to the pattern, the washed-out look of the yellow is part of what adds to the vintage look of the fabric, which is a guaranteed success in these old vans.

Using contrasting fabrics for the back rests added interest and playfulness, but it was important the colours complemented each other and were considered with regards to the big picture. Because Carlene aims for tonality, she likes to create an obvious connection between the back and seat fabrics, but if your intention is more eclectic, you may prefer more contrast between your colours here.

In Goldie, we opted for a vintage-looking fabric for the upholstered seat cushion paired with a solid colour for the back rest. Of course, you have the option to use the same colour fabric for both back rests and seat cushions if you prefer a minimal approach to your scheme, but with so few opportunities to inject colour and pattern in the space, Carlene implores you to reconsider.

Be guided by your overall scheme, step outside the box, and push the limits.

WORKING WITH PATTERNS

Carlene has always been a little bit gun-shy when it comes to using patterns too heavily in her interior designs, out of a concern she would tire of them. Actually, from trial and error she does in fact know that she tires of patterns in her interiors, so her concerns are warranted. It's why she's never ventured down the path of patterned wallpaper, for instance, and instead chooses to focus on elevating a space with colour.

Carlene would be wary of pairing together too many contrasting patterns and colours, as you risk losing the impact of the pattern; however, there are always exceptions. Be guided by your overall scheme. It recently dawned on Carlene that, for the most part, unlike in our home, we simply don't spend enough time in our vans to get tired of anything quickly, so if there were ever an opportunity to step outside your comfort zone with colour and pattern, this is it.

Some pattern is evident in the upholstery and bedding in all our vans, but in Bumblebee and Goldie, Carlene introduced some pattern clashing in the upholstery, pairing two different types of patterns (see image page 68). The key to pulling this off all comes down to scale. Pairing two different patterns of the same scale together can create visual chaos, whereas pairing two patterns of contrasting scales allows you to read each pattern, thereby creating interest. In Bumblebee, Carlene loves the juxtaposition of the angular geometric pattern of the back rest with the soft floral of the seat cushion. It feels unexpected yet very purposeful.

In Goldie, Carlene played on the age of the van by introducing what we coined 'a touch of granny'. The combination of florals and the way they are repeated in different applications (curtains and bench seat) are inspired by our grandparents' homes and how our grandmothers used to decorate. The large-scale vintage look of the floral seat cushion with the solid-coloured backrest is tried and tested, and adding another pattern in the curtain fabric takes it up a notch. It references the colours in the upholstery and some of the other material colours while introducing a new pattern in a smaller scale. The outcome is playful and full of character, which is everything a vintage van should be.

Creating a neutral colour palette – meet Ollie

While Carlene is unwavering and passionate about her love of colour, especially with regards to vintage vans, she appreciates that everyone responds differently to different colours and that some simply prefer a neutral colour scheme. In the context of an interior scheme, neutral colours refer to varying shades of white, cream, beige, black and grey. They're essentially the colours that are omitted from the colour wheel.

If you're a diehard minimalist and can't get on board any use of colour in your van, there are some tools to employ to make a neutral van more cosy, more holiday-like and less 'corporate office'.

Here we feature the van of fellow vintage-van owner Danielle Symes, who resides in Adelaide, Australia, with her husband and two kids. Danielle has renovated a 1982 Windsor Statesmen, called Ollie, primarily employing white, black and tan for an arguably more contemporary and minimalist outcome than our vans.

Sometimes white is a considered choice in design, but sometimes it's employed under the guise of being a safe option. Don't be fooled: white can in fact be one of the most difficult colours to get right. Whites, like all colours, differ significantly in their undertones, and it's something that should be considered in terms of your specific scheme and the quality of light your space receives.

In recent years, black-based whites have been the whites of choice in paint, but umber undertones are hugely effective at softening a white and reducing its starkness. Umber is a reddish-brown colour that, when used in white paint, adds to the saturation level, creating more depth and warmth in the colour. These softer whites are much better suited to classical schemes, as well as in spaces of low light, where they add necessary warmth.

The black accents on the furniture are successful in providing definition and anchoring the neutral surfaces. Without it, white can start to feel washed out and lacking in vibrancy. You don't want your space to feel like it could all start floating away, so to speak.

The pops of tan are also key to the success of this van interior. They add a sense of sophistication and contrast while still remaining faithful to the intended neutrality. The tan also references the warm-coloured timber accents used throughout, such as the rustic timber bench and timber venetian blinds. Carlene believes the timber blinds are a touch of genius in the simplicity of this space. While you might associate timber venetian blinds with the '90s, in here they add warmth and a casualness that feels synonymous with van life, and it just goes to show that context is everything.

SPATIAL PLANNING AND LAYOUT

One of the most important factors to consider when designing the layout of your van is weight distribution. A van that doesn't have proper weight distribution can pose a serious danger on the roads. Too much weight behind the axle will take the weight off the back wheels of the car and can cause the caravan to sway at high speeds, which can lead it to roll over. However, too much weight in front of the axle will put excessive weight on the tow bar and take weight off the front wheels of the car, which can cause loss of steering and control. Ideally, you want to keep the heavy items centred over the axles. This includes items such as refrigerators, cooktops and heavy cabinetry.

By and large, the easiest and most effective way to renovate an old van is to replace old with new. The layout of an original van will have already considered things such as the weight distribution and head heights, and it provides you with a great guide. It's the approach we took with our first four vans. Goldie was the first van for which we conceived a completely new floor plan.

You want to spend a significant amount of time in the planning stage, because unlike something like paint, layout is not something that can be easily changed down the track. Michael makes himself crazy trying to come up with the ultimate layout for our vans, accounting for weight, functionality, best use of storage and aesthetics. We use a 3D render program called SketchUp to draw our floor plans to scale, which we find most useful for workshopping. But you don't need to be a designer or use fancy programs to workshop the ultimate floor plan: using graph paper and pencil can be just as effective. You can purchase graph paper from your local stationery store or office supplier and even download free, printable graph paper online.

HOW TO WORKSHOP YOUR VAN LAYOUT USING GRAPH PAPER

* Accurately measure up the interior footprint of your van. Don't forget about the wheel arches that impede the space, and measure the head height, as this will vary and may affect the position of the bunk beds.

* Draw the outline of your van on your graph paper using a scale in which the outline of the van fills most of the page. Make sure you include the windows and the door.

* Using a separate piece of graph paper and using the same scale, draw and cut out your interior van elements, such as beds, kitchen, wardrobes, seating and tables.

* Move the cut outs around within your van outline until you feel like you've come up with a layout that suits you and your family's needs.

Goldie's spatial planning
with kitchen

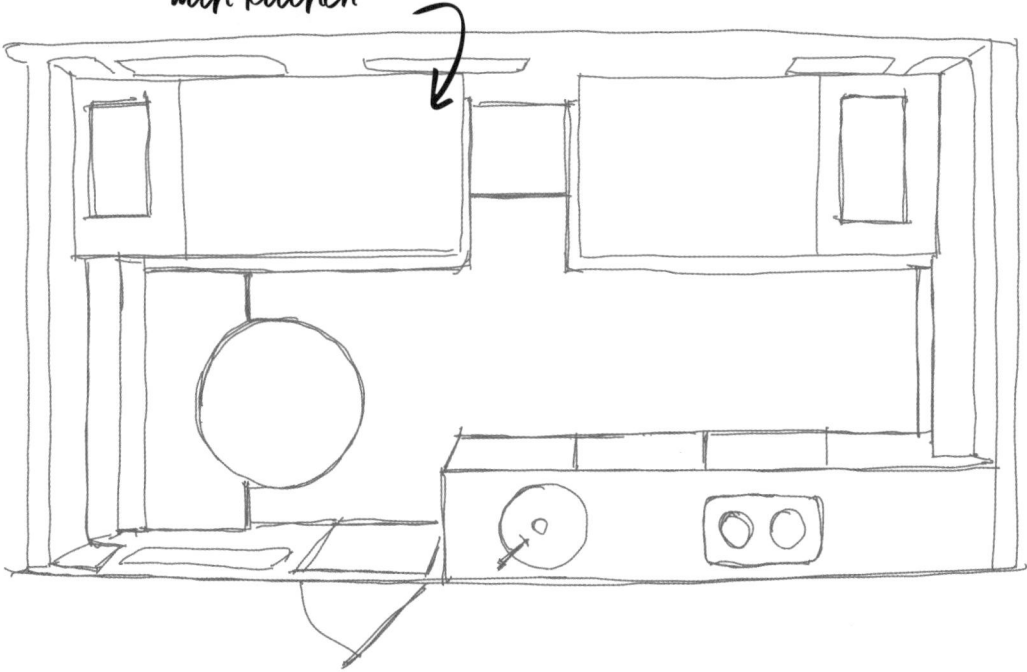

Goldie's spatial planning
with bathroom and kitchen

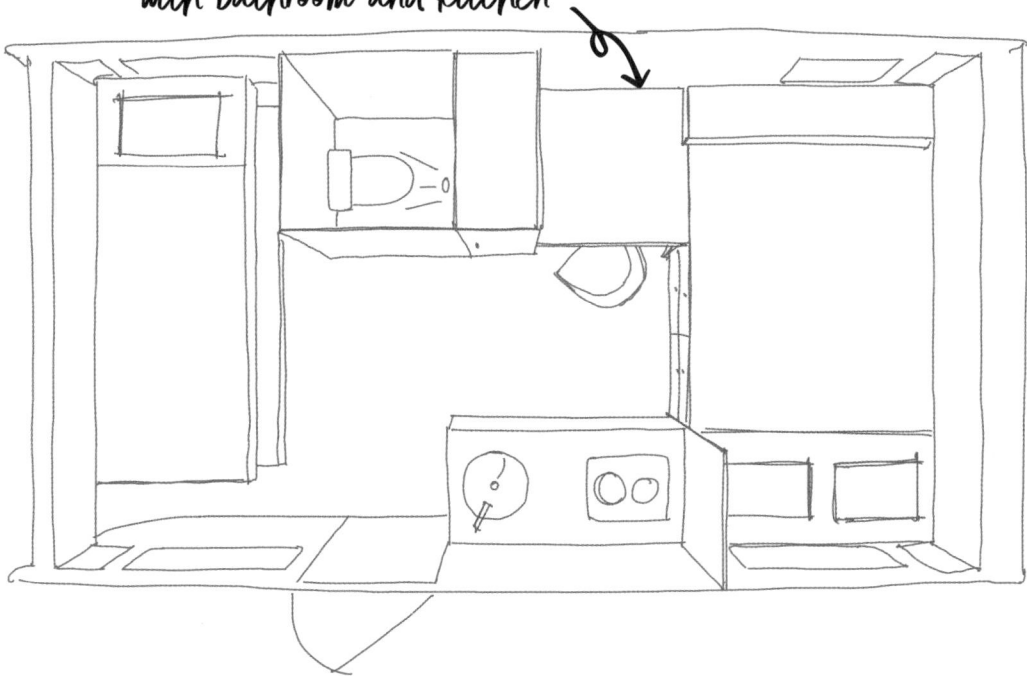

Dolly
BY
CEDAR + SUEDE

BEDS

The beds are going to play a big role in your configuration; so, when conceiving a new van layout, the first thing to decide is how many people you want to sleep comfortably.

In a cosmetic renovation, try to work with what you've got. For example, a common original van layout includes two single beds at one end of the van with a dining table that converts into a bed at the other. If you prefer a bigger bed, a simple and cheap solution is to use a sheet of plywood across the top of the single beds to create a king-size bed, rather than trying to change the entire layout. The gap in between the single beds can be utilised for storage.

Take your cues from the vintage vans and don't be tempted to over-engineer your bunk beds. When you strip back an original van, you realise that there is little to them, and many materials have been selected with consideration of weight reduction. For example, original bunk bed posts are often constructed with little more than 20mm (¾in) aluminium tubing.

Bunks beds can be constructed using lightweight 12mm (½in) plywood and some dressed timber lengths. For the top bunk, we use 112 × 19mm (4½ × ¾in) meranti to construct a frame the size of the mattress. Then, using a router, cut a channel in the timber for the plywood to slot into. Cut the plywood to size and slot it into the frame, gluing all joins. It's a good idea to incorporate some storage under the bottom bunk, so we normally construct a box using meranti framing timber with a hinged top as the bed base.

Placement of the bunk beds can sometimes be difficult. Consider where the existing windows are, where you can get a structural fixing onto the van and the head height of the van. Modern vans generally have higher ceiling heights and can often accommodate three-high bunk beds. We have found that a double bunk in old vans offers a minimum amount of head height in between the bunks. For the sides of the bunks that are not structurally fixed to the van walls, we have used 40mm (1½in) timber dowels, fixed to the frame, as the bed posts.

When we started renovating Millie, the kids were four and six years old, so we opted for bunks above a king-size bed. The beds were at the lower end of the van, and it meant that we and the kids had little headroom, which resulted in a few head bumps in the middle of the night.

As Vonnie was 16ft, we decided on a queen-size bed and opted to employ a dining-table-to-bed conversion for the kids to share. Converted, the bed size was probably about the size of a king single. It turned out to be more practical than first anticipated, especially at our kids' young ages, although we suspect it would be less comfortable for kids over the age of eight years old. We also think that converting the table to bed and back again would start to get old over time.

At 22 ft (6.7m), Dolly gave us the luxury of space, so we installed in a queen-size bed for us and bunk beds for the kids. We were able to divide the sitting area in half to include the bunks with valuable storage underneath. However, the bunks we ended up with in Dolly were actually our second take. Initially, Michael constructed the bunks in a way that the lower bed was semi-enclosed, like a cubbyhole. We road tested it and took the kids on a trip before the interior was painted. Well, they hated it! You can't achieve the optimal head height in a van bunk like you can in a house, and the kids felt too constricted.

Michael obligingly demolished his hard work and instead built standard bunk beds with a simple ladder. The final bunks in Dolly were constructed from 112 × 19mm (4½ × ¾in) pine dressed timber and 12mm ($1^5/_{32}$in) plywood using 40mm (1½in) dowels from the local hardware store and connected with plumbing fittings to introduce the brass accents used throughout.

WARDROBES

The sort of wardrobe space you allow for in your van will come down to the size of the van, the number of people the van needs to accommodate and how you prefer to store your clothes. Carlene likes to hang all her shirts, but pants she'll happily fold. For the rest of the family, she knows for certain they're not going to fold or hang anything. Stella has about four wardrobe changes a day and is in a very frustrating habit of leaving all her clothes wherever they land. Paddy and Michael will put their clothes back in their designated spot, at least, but never neatly.

The bottom line is, Carlene absolutely relies on hanging space, but it need only be kept to a minimum, and she likes to keep everyone else's clothes in drawers.

We take minimal numbers of shoes away on vanning holidays, and we typically store them in a basket under the annex, so that they're not taking up precious interior space. With toiletries, we tend to keep these in baskets of some kind, so that they're easily transported to the caravan park bathroom.

MAXIMISING STORAGE

Creating storage under the beds is without doubt the easiest way of making the most use out of your small space. The most cost-effective way to do this is to put your mattress base on gas struts so you can easily lift the mattress. If you're super handy or have more cash to splash, you might consider large built-in drawers under the beds, but this will also depend on what you're storing. Under our beds we typically store surfboards, the outdoor table and chairs, ladders and other chunky items for which drawers aren't ideal. With Goldie, we had the privilege of five years of vanning experience and had a really good idea of how we wanted the space to function, so for the first time we included storage space that was accessible from the outside of the van.

DINING SPACE

Typically, the dining space in an original vintage van presents as booth seating on either side of a fixed dining table (see also pages 83–4) that is designed to be lowered and converted into a bed. We quickly learned how valuable it is to find a van with a dining table with intact hardware. While we never leave the table in its original condition, van tables don't seem to be readily available to buy as a spare part, and these tables provide a perfect base from which to revamp.

Dolly was the first van in which we used a non-fixed dining table. The table came with the van and folds down for travel. Michael renovated the table base by simply painting it with a brass-look spray paint and made a new top from scratch with plywood topped with laminate.

With Bumblebee, we opted for a very simple approach. We had the benchtop made up in laminate, so we had the table surface done at the same time and reused the original table edging.

KITCHEN DESIGN

In all our vans, and despite their variance in size, we typically locate the kitchen in the centre of the van. The kitchen holds heavy items, such as joinery and the refrigerator, so in terms of achieving even weight distribution, centring the kitchen this way is a good move (for more information see page 72). In addition to achieving weight balance, it also usually just makes the most sense for functionality. The kitchen joinery also provides an easy way to conceal the wheel arch.

CABINET MATERIALS

Cabinet material selection is one of the biggest decisions you will make in a van renovation (second to paint colour). The cabinetry will make up most of what you see in a van and is a chance to inject some character into your build to set your van apart. We've taken a few different approaches to cabinets in our five vans. In Vonnie and Dolly, we simply painted the existing vintage joinery, which is obviously only an option if it's in good condition.

Vintage van cabinet doors are constructed from meranti, skinned on both sides with 3mm (1/10in) plywood. Try to work with what you already have and take your time when removing cupboard doors, reworking them into your new design where you can. If you have to build new doors, use the existing ones as a reference for how they can be constructed. Virtually any laminate finish and colour can be glued to a lightweight plywood substrate. You'll also have the option to have 2-Pac painted cabinet doors, similar to what you see in residential kitchens, but we're not convinced this is an expense worth incurring on your cabinets given the durability of many DIY paints. You can also choose from traditional van building materials, such as veneered plywood or paper foils. If you are a traditionalist and capable of working with timber, the cabinets can be made to match the existing cabinetry. This method might also be necessary if you are just repairing the odd cupboard.

If you're hoping to install a flat-pack kitchen, be mindful that these kitchens are not built with consideration to weight. If you do choose a flat-pack solution, we recommend a light-weight option, as the back panel is constructed from 3mm (1/10in) MDF, rather than the 16mm (5/8in) particleboard that is used in most flat-pack kitchens. For further weight reduction, strategically cut sections out of the sides and backs of standard cabinets, but be careful not to remove any sections where you will need to screw in the drawer runners. Opting for metal drawer sides as opposed to 16mm (5/8in) melamine is another way to keep the van's weight down. Some flat-pack suppliers offer door and drawer fronts in raw materials, which gives you the option to paint them yourself in any colour.

Alternatively, cupboard doors and drawers can simply be cut from 10mm (2/5in) plywood with sections cut out to include a lightweight feature material, such as brass, rattan and acrylic. Chicken wire is another option that offers similar benefits. Get creative.

Another option is to engage a cabinetmaker or joiner. While this is almost certainly the most expensive option, these professionals have access to a large range of materials, and quality professionals will deliver a quality product.

◆◆ ● ◆ ﹐ ◆ ● ● ◆ ● ◆ ●﹐ ◆◆ ◆◆

In Millie, we made a fundamental mistake and demolished *all* of the existing cabinetry, which was in arguably good condition, and replaced it with flat-pack kitchen cabinetry. While the functionality of the kitchen was great, it added unnecessary weight to the van overall, something that could have been avoided.

The cabinetry will make up most of what you see in a van and is a chance to inject some character into your build to set your van apart.

In Dolly, we reused bits of cabinetry that we'd removed to facilitate the installation of a fridge and an oven. The frame was constructed by gluing and stapling meranti that had been skinned on both sides with 3mm (1/10in) plywood. With consideration to weight, we replaced the amber glass inset of the cabinetry with brass mesh.

In Bumblebee, we installed oak cabinet doors but removed the glass fronts and replaced them with rattan. This both added to the overall aesthetic and made for a more lightweight material. Carlene loves this non-solid approaches to cabinet fronts, as they add visual interest and allow us to see through to the items in the cupboards without opening them, while still providing enough concealment that the van didn't appear messy.

A catch is essential on all cupboard doors and drawers in a van. We have arrived at our destination on more than one occasion to a mess of balsamic vinegar that has fallen from an unlocked cupboard. You might be surprised to know that traditional push button locks are still available from caravan spare parts suppliers. Alternatively, if you are removing the original cabinets as part of your renovation, you can consider salvaging the original catches and reuse them. You can also purchase catches from the local hardware store despite the fact they aren't specifically made for vans. These are the option we'd recommend. We've found magnetic catches simply aren't strong enough to securely lock, so avoid them altogether.

COUNTERTOP AND
TABLETOP SURFACES

We made the mistake of choosing form over function in our first vans, in which we tiled the existing table (grout and all) and added a brass edge strip. It looked amazing, but not only did the tile add unnecessary weight; the tables required lowering before transit.

Experience has shown us that laminate is the most suitable choice for a van's countertops, both for its lightweight properties and for durability. It's also a subtle nod to a vintage van's retro origins, although the quality of laminate has come a long way since the '60s and '70s, with more colours and styles available than you probably care to choose from. But don't do what we did in Dolly and choose a gloss laminate finish. A matte finish is much more forgiving. We order laminate directly from a supplier and glue it onto lightweight plywood, but note that many laminate suppliers only supply to trade businesses.

In Mille and Vonnie, we resurfaced the tables with mosaic tiles and edged the table with brass trim, which you can purchase from metal suppliers. The combination is beautiful, but in subsequent vans we opted for laminate tops, which is both light-weight and easy to install. The brass proved to be a real hit and provided a beautiful, subtle pop of luxe.

SPLASHBACK

Tic Tac Tiles are a very good splashback option to use if you have a nice flat surface for them to lay over. They are a stick-on, tile-look product that is lightweight, cost effective, waterproof, simple to install, easy to clean and available in various styles. However, if the wall is uneven due to water damage or has a lot of joins, we recommend another product alltogether, as you won't be able to hide the imperfections. In this case, a laminate splashback is a very good option, and if you are having a laminate bench and tabletop made, you might as well do your splash at the same time.

In Bumblebee we used the same material for the splashback as the benchtop, which was lightweight plywood with a laminate laid upon it. This is something we'll continue to do going forward.

APPLIANCES, FIXTURES AND FITTINGS

There are a few ways to approach the appliances in your caravan, and for the most part, the choices may come down to your budget. Specific caravan appliances are refined and designed to meet the specific needs of van life, but they're also expensive, so ask yourself a few hard questions about how you intend to use the van.

SINKS

Most household sinks can be used in vans. We've sourced our sinks from either eBay or van parts suppliers. Stainless steel is the most suitable option for a van because it's lightweight, durable and easy to install. Avoid porcelain sinks, as they are heavy and more susceptible to damage. A small round sink seems to be the best option in the modest space that is a van interior. We've also found it helpful to use a sink that comes with a chopping board cut out to add to that precious bench space. In particularly small vans, consider omitting a sink inside completely; you might be better off using a plastic bucket for washing dishes outside or doing the washing up at the communal kitchen if you're at a caravan park.

MICROWAVES

If you choose to include a microwave in your van, we recommend keeping it small. We only use a microwave sporadically and could get away without including one at all, but we also take our coffee machine away on holidays, which is a clue to the kind of campers we are. In Millie, we included a microwave that was larger than we really needed for that small space, whereas in Dolly, we carried a light, small-scale model that took up little space in our kitchen cabinets and could be very easily removed. In Goldie, we've omitted one all together.

TAPS

To Carlene, the style of the kitchen tap you choose says a lot about the type of aesthetic you're trying to achieve. In all of our vans, we've used traditional kitchen mixers to keep with our overarching schemes. If you want your van interior to reflect a modern look and feel, something with cleaner lines will better reflect that style.

Traditional

The ornate profile lends itself to a traditional-style interior. Its details reflect a sense of quirkiness that feels very fitting to a vintage van.

Classic

A gooseneck is a classic style of tap that could easily slip into any van aesthetic. The simple, no-fuss design makes it incredibly versatile. It is often Carlene's go-to in a home interior.

Modern

The angular lines of this style of tap lend themselves to a modern van aesthetic. The squad height makes this tap squad a relatively compact option, which might be a consideration for you in the small space of a van.

In all of our vans, we've used traditional kitchen mixers to keep with our overarching schemes.

REFREGERATORS

In three of our five vans, we used two-way fridges by Dometic that run on both 12V and 240V/110V. Even though we do all of our caravanning on powered sites in caravan parks, the 12V component gives us the capacity to travel off-grid should we need it (for more information see page 111). This option also is better for resale.

Note that these fridges require a vent at the rear for the hot air to escape (see the illustrations below).

The advantages of using a van-specific fridge are:

✳ They are designed to be installed and fixed to the van.

✳ They come with an installation surround for a seamless finish.

✳ They can be latched for travel.

✳ They automatically switch between 12V and 240V/110V.

✳ They can be opened on the left or right at your discretion to fit preference and design.

✳ Some have drains that can be connected to a tube under the van, making the fridge easy to clean.

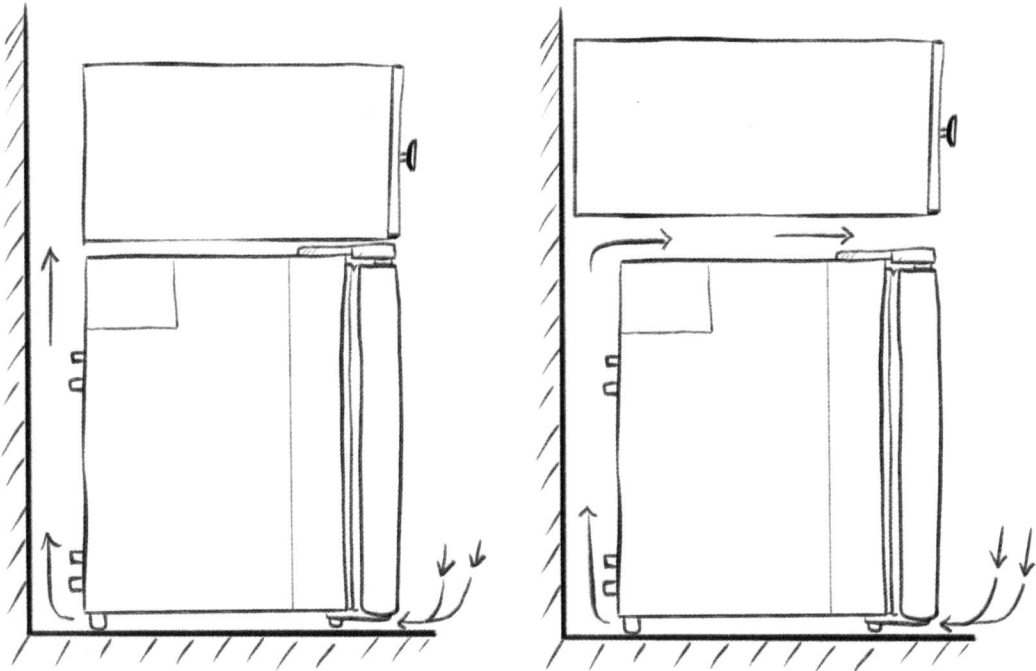

The above illustrations show two examples of how a fridge can be vented but appliances should always be vented as per the specific installation instructions.

Gas stoves

RV-specific gas stoves have been our go-to when it comes to stoves in our vans. These stoves are recessed into the bench and have a glass lid that protects your splashback when opened and provides precious extra bench space when closed.

Not all stoves are created equal, and some household gas stoves are not suitable for installation in a van. RV stoves must be fitted with a flame-failure device that stops the flow of gas should the flame go out. Gas appliances should also be low pressure, operating at or below 2.75 kPa.

Electric and induction cooktops

For those committed to powered-only vanning, it is worth considering a portable electric or induction cooktop. These are inexpensive and can be stowed away when not in use to free up valuable bench space. A portable electric cooktop was our cooktop of choice for the pull-out kitchen in Goldie.

PULL-OUT EXTERNAL KITCHEN

Thinking about what works for you and your family's habits is key to coming up with a solution for your own specific needs.

In our most recent van, Goldie, we did something completely different to the rest of our fleet, but something that we feel works for us and how we function in our van. We designed the kitchen to pull out from the exterior of the van, so that all cooking could happen outside and better use could be made of the inside space for sleeping and storage.

To fit the pull-out kitchen, we raised the main bed on the inside of the van, which gave us plenty of space to create a functional kitchen underneath. We installed large hatches to utilise every square inch of the storage underneath the bed. The main kitchen bench is positioned across the width of the van and slides out into the back of the annex. Having it slide out on this end was an intentional decision, as we didn't want it to ruin our 'streetscape' and our connection to all that is happening around us, which would have been the case had it pulled out from the front of the van. When the kitchen is out, a hatch on the other side of the van gives us access to that space for storage during our stay. No storage space goes unused on camping trips.

In this particular set-up, we opted for a small domestic fridge, rather than a specific camping or caravan fridge. We stay at powered sites, so the fridge is secured in the van while travelling and lives under our annex for easy access once we get set up. It might sound unconventional but this is what works for us, and thinking about what works for you and your family's habits is key to coming up with a solution for your own specific needs.

Workshopping Goldie's layout

Interestingly, Goldie, our most recent vintage belle, provided our biggest layout challenge. After five years of vanning, we had the benefit of experience on our side, but she was also a complete strip-out, so we almost had too many options. We workshopped many iterations of a floor plan before settling on one that works for us and how we want to function in our van. We designed and redesigned and started building to a 'final' design, only to change the design again. Anyone who's renovated a van will tell you it's nothing like renovating a house, and you need to be prepared to make changes on the fly. Let us walk you through our thought process.

Below are the whopping six floor plans we considered for Goldie. In all cases, the kitchen pulls out from the outside of the van (for more information see page 101), meaning we were able to free up space inside and also create a camp-style kitchen. For us that means the first person up in the morning can go and put the kettle on without risking waking up the entire family. We've also found that with the kitchen inside, we're inclined to feel a bit cooped up during meal preparation, when we have so much more space to utilise outside, where all the action is.

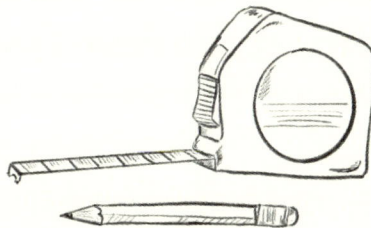

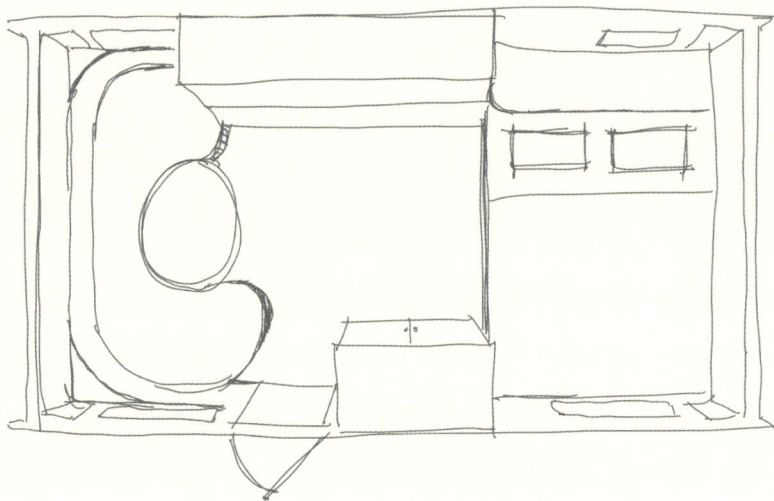

OPTION 1

Floor plan 1 includes a queen-size bed, which is the minimum size we are comfortable sleeping on. In this plan, the tall joinery houses fold-down bunk beds for the kids that we would pull down at night and fold back up in the morning. They're commonly called Murphy beds, named after the inventor,

William Lawrence Murphy. Michael really liked the idea of a chunky, curved sofa with a little cafe table that was not fixed in its location. The tall cabinet is a wardrobe that would serve Michael and Carlene, and the kids' clothes would be stored in drawers under the queen-size bed.

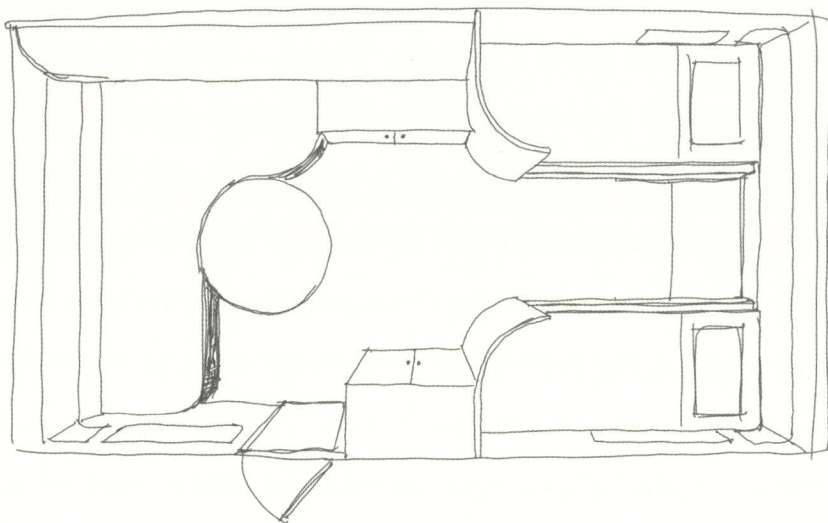

OPTION 2

Layout 2 was a serious contender. Moving the bunks to one end of the van meant we could hang a curtain to separate the sleeping area from the living space. In this floor plan, we shortened the cabinet and

created slightly more seating by curving the bench seat, ultimately adding to its size. Aesthetically, we liked the curve of the sofa, but it would compromise the capacity for drawers beneath it.

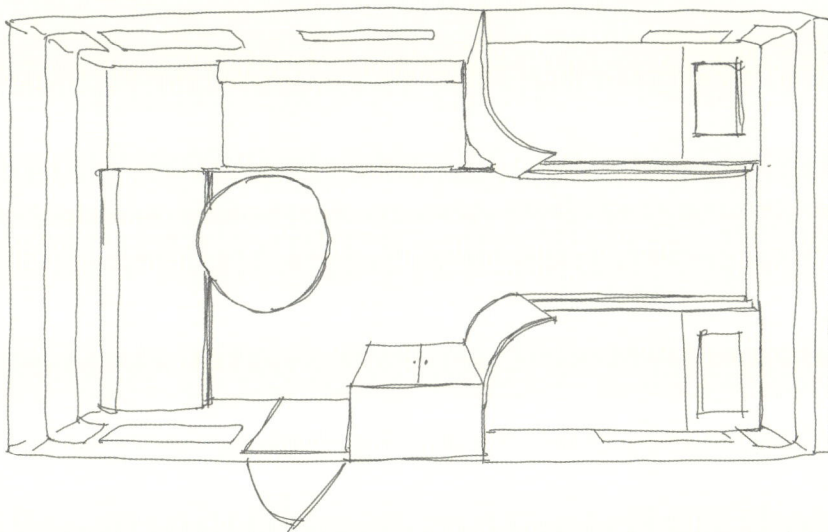

OPTION 3

This option completely eliminates the waist-height bench, making the seating area feel super generous and quite inviting. We'd also have no trouble including drawers under the bench in this scenario.

However, at this point Michael started to question whether the four bunk beds would allow for enough space to store the outdoor pull-out kitchen.

OPTION 4

Completely flipping the floor plan on its head, this iteration reintroduces the queen-size bed, raising it to allow for plenty of room underneath to store the pull-out kitchen. Carlene loved the exposed hanging rail, as she prefers to hang her clothes

rather than folding them. The tall, narrow cupboard opposite looks awkward against the curve of the bunk bed and feels a bit like it's been jammed into the corner. We were getting there with this option, but it still needed work.

OPTION 5

Michael conceded that curves and organic shapes require the luxury of space, which is something we absolutely do not have in a van. Squaring off all the joinery eliminates dead space and generally feels less forced. The bench seat is a flex space for eating, board games, reading and whipping out the laptop, as we're begrudgingly sometimes forced to do even on holidays. At 60cm (23½in) diameter, the small round table is therefore less a dining table and more what we like to call a cafe table.

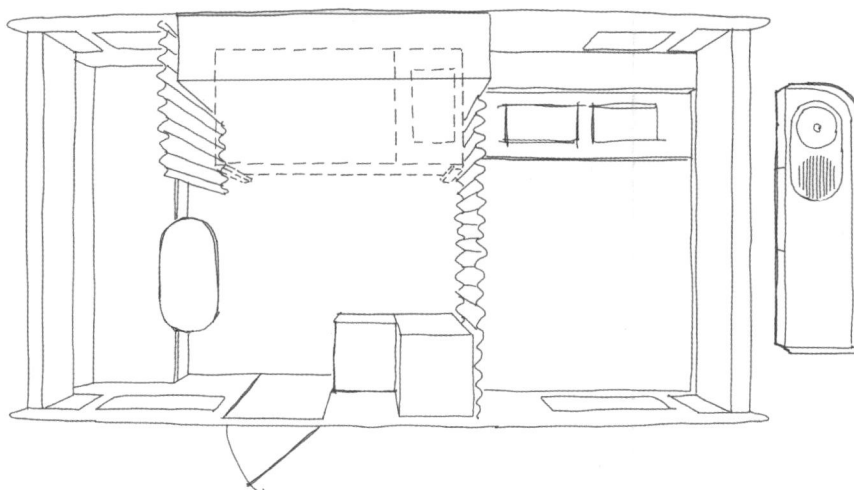

THE FINAL FLOOR PLAN

Michael had already started building when he flipped the floor plan once again. The sixth and final iteration saw the Murphy bunks from the original layout reinstated. The bench seat was given the full width of the van, making it a more functional sitting area, and we scored the most perfect free-standing vintage wardrobe from Facebook Marketplace, which not only fit the space perfectly but is incredibly lightweight, a key consideration for vanning materials. It also saved Michael a truckload of work in having to construct something from scratch.

Max and Karstan's VW Kombi van – meet The GOAT

Our mates Max and Karstan have recently set out on the adventure of a lifetime. They are travelling our wild and untamed island nation (Australia) full-time in their beloved 1968 VW Kombi panel van with their adventurous four-year-old daughter, Zuri. Like a caravan, travelling and living out of a Kombi van requires smart storage solutions, weight considerations and functionality. Karstan refuses to give the van a name but said we can call it The GOAT (The Greatest Of All Time) for the purposes of this book. (Michael wants to call it Rust Bucket!)

We love how, while some Kombi travellers prefer to restore their vans with a fresh paint job and sleek interior, Max and Karstan have embraced the rustic aesthetic of their van. Instead, they've

placed emphasis on ensuring their van functions in a way that provides them with exactly what they need on the road and nothing more.

Max and Karstan had ventured on enough short trips to know what improvements they needed to make to their van for full-time life on the road. These included:

* custom-built 21.1cc engine

* 3½in (9cm) lift

* 32in (81cm) mud-terrain tyres

* slide-out functional kitchen with a gas cooktop

* storage unit behind the seating area with a sink

* slide out 90l (23.76gal) dual-zone fridge and freezer

* 200Ah lithium batteries with a 100W inverter.

Karstan's mechanical experience, love and knowledge of VW Kombi vans and overall handiness mean he's equipped to tackle the issues that inevitably arise when an old van meets the rugged terrain of Australia's outback.

There are a few items that Maxine and Karstan travel with that they've found makes life on the road a bit easier. These include:

* awning tent for extended stays, which keeps their daughter, Zuri, from wandering off

* battery-powered blower, which the couple use for cleaning and for keeping the fire burning

* GPS satellite phone and tracker. This is important for safety and allows friends and family to track their movements

* UHF radio

* 12V oven, which is very useful for heating up leftovers

* custom-made flyscreens and flyscreen doors.

Life on the road in a vintage Kombi takes a certain attitude – a thirst for adventure, a penchant for the unexpected and the capacity to do it a little rough with an open heart. Or maybe life on the road perpetuates this mentality. We've no doubt it comes with challenges, but witnessing Max and Karstan's adventures makes us want to pack my bags and leave it all our behind in a cloud of red dust.

ELECTRICAL

Not dissimilar to designing a home's electrical requirements, careful planning is necessary to ensure your van not only looks the part but functions to your needs. Before you start running cables, spend some time visualising how you intend to use the van.

Electrical systems for vans range dramatically in price, and the system you choose to install should be determined by the type of vanning you plan to undertake and your budget.

WARNING

All electrical work involving mains power supply (240V/110V) *must* be completed by a licensed electrician and adhere to strict regulations specific to your country and state.

THE CONVENIENCE CAMPERS

If you plan on *only* using your van at powered sites, then you could have it wired to use only 240V/110V (similar to your house).

PROS:

* cheaper lighting and appliances with more options to choose from

* simple solution

* cheaper set-up costs.

CONS:

* requires powered sites

* difficult to upgrade to a 12V system later

* could reduce resale price

* could limit your resale market.

THE OFF-GRID TRAVELLERS

A standard off-grid system will consist of batteries, solar panels, battery chargers and inverters. It's worth getting a specialist to design your system, as your requirements and, more importantly, budget will be specific to you and your needs.

PROS:

* the world is your oyster: go anywhere!

* environmentally friendly option

* increase in resale price

* inverters can provide 240V/110V power.

CONS:

* more expensive initial set-up costs

* fewer, and generally more expensive, 12V appliances available

* adds weight to your van.

HOW MUCH ENERGY WILL MY CARAVAN NEED?

We recommend speaking with a van battery specialist who can recommend a battery/solar set-up specific to your energy needs.

Appliance	Energy usage
LED lights and battery monitoring devices	Less than 0.5A per hour
Water pumps and tank level monitoring	Less than 0.5A per hour
Small fridge	1–3A per hour
Large fridge	3–5A per hour
Small electronic devices (small TV, laptop, music player, etc.)	Less than 0.5A per hour
Charging mobile devices	Less than 0.5A per hour

THE READY-FOR-ANYTHING CAMPERS

Not sure what style of travelling you plan on doing? A simple combination of a 12V battery, a battery charger and mains power (240V/110V) could be the perfect in-between solution. All lights and appliances are 12V and run off the battery, and the power points are the only mains power in the van.

PROS:

✶ possible to upgrade with solar panels and more

✶ less expensive than full off-grid to set-up initially.

CONS:

✶ still requires dual-powered appliances (12V or 240V/110V) or a 12V to 240V/110V inverter system.

12V SET-UPS

Depending on how and where you camp, you may want to consider installing a solar system as either a backup to or in addition to , your 12V or 240V/110V set-up. First, assess the amount of energy you may need for your van.

A typical 12V battery will provide 100Ah of power. This means that the battery should be able to provide 1A of power for 100 hours (or 2A for 50 hours, 5A for 20 hours, etc.).

BATTERIES

Batteries have come a long way in recent years. An AGM deep cycle battery was the only option for a long while; however, lithium batteries are now a great option.

Lithium batteries are smaller, lighter and have a better depth of discharge. This means that a lithium battery has a higher percentage of usable amp hours than an AGM. For example, a 200Ah lithium battery might provide 160Ah of usable power, whereas an equivalent AGM battery only gives eq. 100Ah before needing to be recharged.

Lithium batteries are more expensive than AGM batteries but they also have twice the life span. Poor person pays twice. A disadvantage of lithium batteries is that most can't be used as cranking batteries.

Typically, the batteries are installed under bench seats or in the front locker of caravans.

BATTERY BOXES

Battery boxes are inexpensive and are a great way to store and secure the battery. They allow for easy electrical connection and often have built-in isolation switches and Anderson plugs for connection of solar power or for the battery to power other appliances, such as external fridges, directly.

BATTERY CHARGERS

A simple way to charge the battery is to use a battery charger plugged into the power outlet adjacent to the battery. Be sure to use a charger that has the capacity to charge your specific type of battery. Some chargers are interchangeable with various types of batteries and others are only compatible with a single type.

12V BATTERIES WITH SOLAR POWER

Considered the most popular option for vans, a 12V deep cycle battery delivers sufficient power to keep basic 12V appliances and other electrical items powered. You will need solar panels with a 12V rating of up to 200W. A 200W panel can generate around 60Ah per day in ideal weather conditions, and with that, you can charge a 100Ah battery in 5–8 hours. It's important to know that your battery will require a minimum voltage to operate appliances. This means that the average deep cycle battery will need to be at least 50 per cent charged to run your appliances. A single 200W panel can charge a 12V battery in a day, but the smaller the solar panel, the longer the charging time. You can also recharge your battery from a mains power supply.

SOLAR SET-UPS

Several variables affect the amount of energy that solar panels will generate:

* time of year

* weather

* location

* type of charge controller.

To determine the type of system you'll need, consider the components of a solar set-up for a van and the options available. There are four major components in a solar set-up that you need to know about before installation:

* solar panels

* regulator

* battery (see page 112)

* inverter.

Types of solar panels for vans

There are three main types of solar panels suitable for vans:

Glass solar panels: These are the most common and established solar panels for vans today. They come with a rigid frame that is attached to the roof and are typically used for household and commercial installations.

Mobile solar panels: These are lightweight and semi-flexible, making them more expensive than glass solar panels. They can be added directly onto a curved roof using silicone, without the need for mounting brackets.

Folding solar panels: These solar panels are gaining popularity in the van world due to the fact that there is no mounting required. They can be easily manoeuvred around the space to maximise their exposure to sunlight, thereby maximising the energy captured.

Installing solar panels: The easiest way to install solar for your van is to purchase a preconfigured solar panel kit, which comes with all the necessary parts. A typical solar panel kit includes at least two solar panels, a charge controller, a regulator mounting brackets to fit the panels to the caravan's roof, cables, fuses and connectors. You will find that most solar panel kits don't come with a battery or an inverter, so these will need to be purchased separately.

INVERTERS

Many large appliances, such as air conditioners, require 240V/110V power. An inverter will take the 12V DC power from your van's battery and covert it into 240V/110V.

There's a big range of inverters on the market at a wide range of price points. A basic inverter usually starts at around 100W, but they can go up to 6000W. If you intend to be on the road for more than a few days at a time, you will need a high-quality inverter. It will cost you more upfront but will save you money in the long run.

12V SWITCH PANELS

These switch panels come in all shapes and sizes and are pre-wired for easy installation. Some have an inbuilt voltage meter and are overload protected by a separate circuit breaker. They are easy to install (using appropriate crimp connectors or lugs, see page 116) and are relatively inexpensive. Most switches come with identification stickers so you can see what each is used for.

FUSE BOXES

The individual circuits should be protected by fuses to protect the wiring. The fuse box can be installed on the electrical board for easy access to the fuses should they need to be replaced. The fuses should be sized based on the rating on the wires used and the load required.

CABLE

It's important to use the correct size cables when wiring your van, as these wires will be hidden in the walls of the van, and it's a difficult mistake to fix if you get it wrong.

The size of the 12V wires required depends on the load placed on the circuit and the length of the cable. For a small, simple system, a 12V automotive twin core cable (often called a figure 8) of 3–6mm ($\frac{1}{10}$–$\frac{1}{4}$in) should be sufficient to run the lights and pumps. For more complex systems, it's best to get an auto electrician, regular electrician or specialist to calculate the size required.

When running the electrical feed for appliances, refer to the installation instructions for the specific cable size required. If the correct cable size is not used, there could be a significant voltage drop between the battery and the appliance, potentially large enough for the appliance not to work at all.

Unless using non-migratory cable (usually blue or purple), ensure that the cabling is not in contact with any polystyrene insulation, as over time the insulation makes the outer cable insulation brittle, which can break and expose the wires. In caravans with metal frames, nylon bushes or grommets should be installed in the cable holes to protect the cables from sharp edges.

If the van is timber framed, avoid drilling holes for cables in a row at equal heights, as this can affect the structural integrity of the frame. A dab of silicon on the cable where it passes through the frame will secure it and protect it from rubbing and exposing bare cables.

Be cautious about choosing to reuse any existing wiring, as it may not comply with current regulations. Who knows what changes a DIY electrician has made in past renovations? Make sure a licensed electrician thoroughly checks any existing cables.

ELECTRICAL CRIMP CONNECTOR KITS

The easiest way to install 12V connections is to use a crimp connector kit. These kits are inexpensive to purchase and easy to use. Simply strip the insulation off the last 15mm (⅝in) of the electrical wire, twist and fold the stripped part in half and push it into the terminal. Use a crimper to fasten the connector onto the wire, and give the wire a little pull to ensure a good connection.

POWER OUTLETS

We've been caught out too many times with an insufficient number of power points, so trust us when we say it's a good idea to write a list of all locations that you want a power outlet. Once the build is complete, installing new power outlets will be difficult and may compromise your design.

Consideration should be given to:

* appliances, such as fridge, microwave, coffee machine and TV (if you dare install one)

* add plenty above the benchtops in the kitchen. Be aware of minimum distances required from sinks.

* external requirements, such as a switchable power points for festoon lighting around the annex

* by the beds for charging phones, watches, etc.

* USB outlets

* power for the battery charger.

ELECTRICAL BOARD

The position of the electrical board also needs to be factored into your design. The electrical board will contain all your circuit breakers, fuses, isolation switches, hot-water control, water tank levels and the like. Additionally, off-grid systems that include batteries, chargers and inverters can take up a lot of room and should be considered in the design phase of the project. This board must be easily accessible and unimpeded (that is, it cannot be installed at the back of a wardrobe). We typically locate ours in an overhead cupboard.

All power outlets must be double pole switched, meaning that both the active and the neutral are switched for added safety.

240V/110V SET-UPS

All mains power electrical work *must* be done by a licensed electrician. Government rules and regulations vary from country to country (even state to state) and are continually changing, so it's imperative that a professional completes the work. The following information is generic and is only designed to help you purchase the correct parts. It's the responsibility of the licensed electrician to ensure the installation abides by local regulations.

COMPONENTS

The mains power inlet should be a 15A male plug rated for external use and with a weatherproof cover. These are available at most electrical supplier outlets. The 15A inlet has a larger earth pin to ensure a regular 10A power lead cannot be plugged into it. Always use a 15A lead.

It's a legal requirement to install a safely switch on all 240V/110V circuits. Any large appliances, such as air conditioners, typically require a separate circuit breaker.

OUR PREFERRED ELECTRICAL SET-UP

In our preferred design in the illustration below, the battery is charged by a charger that is plugged into a power outlet installed next to the battery. The battery then feeds a switch panel, which allows each circuit to be isolated. The switch panel supplies power to the individual feeds through a fuse box. Generally, we divide our power feeds into different components, such as lights, fridge, water pump and range hood. If you have more than one light feed, they could all be connected to the one switch in the switch panel provided they do not draw too much current.

240V/12V Electrical Schematic
scale 1:20

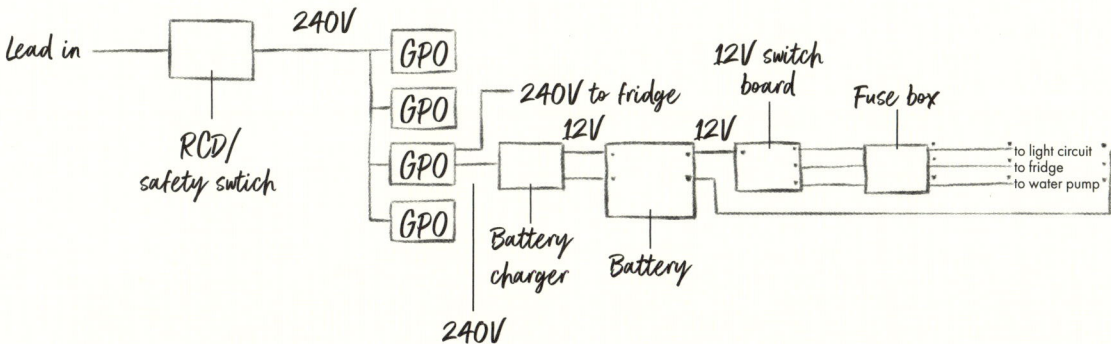

Lead in — 240V — GPO — GPO — GPO — GPO

RCD/ safety switch

240V

Battery charger

240V to fridge

12V

Battery

12V switch board

12V

Fuse box

to light circuit
to fridge
to water pump

LIGHTING

Vans are small spaces and don't require a lot of lighting. Ideally, you should install 12V lights. Many light fittings can accept 12V light bulbs but will require a transformer to power the light. Concealed LED lighting is often a great solution, as it offers a good amount of lighting, is easy to install and adds ambience.

When using 240V/110V light fittings, any fitting with exposed terminals with the bulb removed will not be suitable (and is illegal). Note that the electrical code in some countries even prohibits electricians from installing such lights in homes at a height lower than 180cm (71in).

Ask yourself what type of lighting you expect to use – for example, strip lighting, reading lights, task lights (usually required in the kitchen) or nightlights.

This is also the time to consider external lights. While most new vans provide a single external wall light, generally this doesn't give enough light for all the things we want to do in the annex, like playing board games, eating and drinking. A switchable external power point can be installed to allow for festoon lighting to be strung up around the perimeter of the annex, which creates a festive, carnival vibe that feels very in keeping with a vintage caravan.

Contrary to first hunches, going large in small spaces doesn't necessarily make a space feel smaller. In fact, the opposite is true. In the case of the giant pendants used for Millie and Bumblebee, they created a sense of drama, a focal point and a bit of the unexpected. The large pendants work because they're woven and not solid, therefore keeping the space both literally and visually light. A solid material may not have had the same success. Needless to say, the shades come down while travelling, and we only put them back up when we're at our destination.

In Vonnie, we kept our lighting more minimal and opted for a combination of concealed LED strip lighting and a simple vintage aesthetic.

In Goldie, we exclusively used a combination of different wall lights. We didn't require any task lighting inside, given we'd located the kitchen outside.

◆ ● ◆ ● ◆ ● ◆ ● ◆ ● ◆ ● ◆ ◆

In Dolly, we did away with all decorative lights and ran an LED strip light around the shadow line of the perimeter of the ceiling, which we had battened out and re-sheeted (see the illustration below). This provided both a good amount and quality of light without it being too in your face. What we don't like about Dolly's lighting is that there are no localised lights. We really need reading lights with a nearby switch, so someone can read without disturbing the rest of the family.

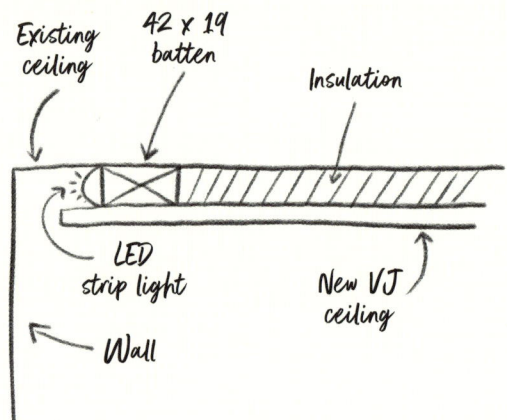

With our first girl Millie, Michael told Carlene that as long as the cupboard doors could open unhindered by a light fixture, she could choose whatever she wanted. Well, he was not prepared for the size of pendant she came home with.

LIGHT SWITCHES

You need to consider the location of the light switches early in the planning process. We strongly recommend having a good think about the locations in advance of the electrician turning up to do their job, and even do a basic electrical plan if you think it helps. Carlene has a history of being put on the spot and making poor decisions about the placement of light switches, so we can say with certainty that you'll kick yourself for not being prepared. You'll also need to decide if the switches should be two-way switched, which means the light can be turned on and off from more than one switch point.

If using a 12V lighting system, any household switch is suitable, which means there is a huge selection to choose from. Many suppliers are also still making traditional-style switches, which look very fitting in these old vans. You only need to Google 'traditional light switch' to be presented with a huge range in various metal finishes. On the flip side, you might also deem this a good place to cut costs and opt for an inexpensive option from the hardware store.

However, if using a 240V/110V system, all switches must be double poled, meaning both the active and the neutral conductors are switched for added safety. This will limit the switch options available to you.

TRAILER LIGHTS

Specific trailer wire is available from most electrical suppliers. We suggest using a seven-core cable. This cable uses standard colours for wiring to the trailer plugs and is required if brakes are to be installed (see the illustration below). A five-core cable is sufficient if brakes are not required (for more information see page 33) are either 7 pin round or 7 pin flat and are easily fitted by following the wiring diagram supplied with the plug. Adapters between flat and round plugs are also available to accommodate cars installed with a different socket.

To determine the minimum light requirements for your van, consult local regulations, as each state and country will have very specific requirements.

In Australia (see the photo below), vans require:

✱ rear position lamps (red)

✱ front position lamps (red), only required if your van is wider than 5.2ft (1.6m) and longer than 13.1ft (4m) or if the van is wider than 5.9ft (1.8m), irrespective of length

✱ rear stop lamps

✱ direction indicator lamps

✱ registration plate lamp

✱ forward-facing side marker (amber), only required if your van is wider than 6.9ft (2.1m). This can be a combination light with the rear position light.

Direction indication lamp

Position lamp/side marker combo

Rear registration plate lamp

Rear stop lamps/ Rear position lamp combo (tail lights)

AIR CONDITIONING

Air conditioners come in many shapes and sizes. The most common types suitable for vans are roof mounted and can weigh up to 40kg (88lb). Before installation, ensure the roof has sufficient strength to support the weight of the air conditioner, both while stationary and in transit. Pre-fabricated brackets are available and can be installed on top of the van to distribute the weight to the external walls. If the van is completely stripped out, the roof structure can be strengthened using aluminium rectangle sections. Alternatively, if there is no roof space left or the roof isn't strong enough, you can opt for a unit that can be installed underneath a bed or bench. Another consideration to the placement is weight distribution throughout the van.

The size of the opening is important when fitting an air conditioner to an old caravan and may determine the model you choose. The air conditioner should be placed as centrally as possible in the van and face the direction of travel. If the van is longer than 23ft (7m) you might want to consider installing two units.

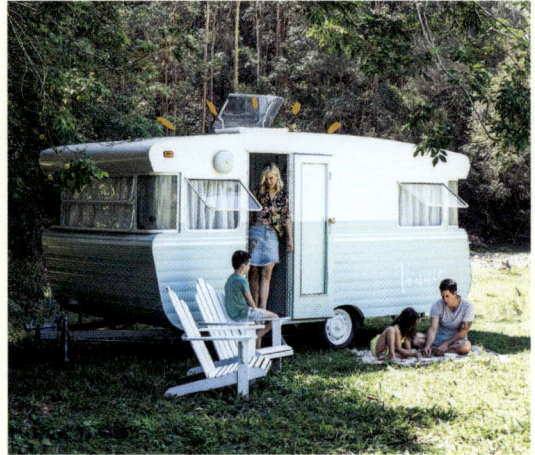

ROOF HATCHES

In Vonnie and Goldie, we installed a specific RV roof hatch from a RV parts supplier that also came with a solid blind and fly screen, making it super functional. To install an RV roof hatch, adhere to the instructions supplied for your specific model. In our other vans, we simply utilised existing roof hatches and added a new gas strut mechanism. We've found this approach both very cost effective and practical for letting in light and achieving airflow.

Goldie was the first van in which we considered installing an air conditioning unit. We've never travelled anywhere cold enough to need heating, and in our previous vans we've always just used desk fans when it's been hot enough to warrant it.

Cassette toilets come with a removal component for waste emptying at dump points provided by van parks.

SHOWERS AND TOILETS

Except for a simple outdoor shower that attaches to the exterior of the van, we've decided against including a bathroom in all five of our vans. In Australia, original vans generally don't include toilets, and given we specifically holiday in caravan parks, often with ensuite sites (What can we say? We're glampers), we've always felt that for us personally, a van bathroom would compromise the space more than it would add value. This is just something everyone needs to evaluate against their specific needs and circumstances.

The good news is that if you decide a van bathroom would make van life better, it's simpler than it sounds. Many suppliers of van parts offer complete bathroom cubicles. The simplest approach is to source a premade, one-piece fibreglass shower cubicle. Alternatively, you can purchase a fibreglass shower base and build your own walls, lining them with laminate and using silicone to seal the joins.

The benefit of the all-in-one cubicle is that you won't have to worry about leaks that can potentially emerge in the joins over time.

In the spatial planning phase of the design, it's important to position the bathroom in a spot where the drain is not impeded by any major structural elements of the trailer.

Van toilets can be purchased from any van part supplier. Some suppliers offer one-part fibreglass shower cubicles moulded with toilet plinths to fit specific van toilets. Cassette toilets (that come with a removal component for waste emptying at dump points) must be mounted on an exterior wall with an external service door to allow for easy removal of the waste cassette for emptying. We suggest placing the toilet on the side opposite the entry door, so you don't have to access it via the annex when you empty the cassette. Think of the non-annex side of the van as your utility space.

HARD FINISHES
AND MATERIALS

Material selection is everything when it comes to
caravan renovations, and factors such as weight,
durability and moisture resistance should be
considered in the material selection process.

WALL PANELLING

The most cost-effective approach to your wall panelling is to simply restore and paint what's already there, subject to its condition, of course. If you're tempted to include some sort of wall panelling for a bit of added interest, just ensure it is lightweight. The MDF sheet panels that you can buy off the shelf from your local hardware supplier are too heavy, which is unfortunate as it would definitely be the simplest option. The VJ panelling we've used on the ceilings of some of our vans was custom made from 5mm (³⁄₁₆in) plywood. We engaged a local timber supplier to cut the vertical grooves into the sheets 100mm (4in) apart.

Another product used for wall cladding and ceiling applications is paper or polyester overlay plywood, which comes in 2.7mm (⁷⁄₆₄in) or 3.6mm (⁹⁄₆₄in) sheets and a range of prefinished colours. Some renovators are using aluminium composite (such as SAS Econ-Panel) or wet area panels, which are high-pressure melamine panels; however, with both these types of panels you lose a bit of character, and they can be aesthetically cold.

Back in the day, and still today, caravan makers use meranti in both the walls and the cabinet frames. It's strong, light and easy to use, and frames can be made using PVA glue and an industrial staple gun to join them. Avoid using standard framing timber to build walls and bunks and the like – it's simply too heavy for towing.

Material selection is everything when it comes to caravan renovations, and factors such as weight, durability and moisture resistance should be considered when selecting your materials.

CABINET DOORS

The material you use to construct your cabinet doors will be governed by whether or not you are trying to match what is there, but we generally use lightweight plywood, which we also use to construct benchtops, doors and the framing under the beds. The traditional Viscount doors use a 3mm (1/10in) face with a meranti frame and a 3mm (1/10in) back.

In Goldie, the sidewall cladding was in acceptable condition, but the front and back lower panels were damaged beyond repair. It didn't help that Michael put a bobcat bucket through the front wall when trying to move the van. In this instance we decided to replace those panels, but it's not a cheap undertaking.

CLADDING

Cladding is the material or covering applied to the outside of a structure. Trying to match van cladding is nearly impossible. If you're lucky, you might be able to find a similar model at a scrap yard from which to salvage enough cladding for your purpose. Alternatively, if you can't replace or repair the cladding, you may be able to cover the imperfections using a strategically placed vent or access panel.

Except for one side, Dolly's exterior was in relatively good condition. The previous owner informed us that during a storm one night, the tent-pole tips had damaged the cladding, resulting in over 100 annoying little dents, but our auto painter managed to fill most of them prior to painting. If you are doing your own painting, use autobody-grade filler to repair any little dents or holes during the paint preparations.

If you're able to retain any of the original hardware from the original van, do it.

HARDWARE

Hardware refers to things such as door handles, cabinet knobs, hinges, brackets and hooks. If you're able to retain any of the original hardware from the van, do it. You'll be surprised how the costs of these little items can add up when you buy them new. Besides, the original hardware is typically loaded with character and soul, which is hard to reproduce. If you do need to source new handles, do it with your aesthetic scheme in mind. In the past, we've preferred to pay tribute to the vans' origins by opting for ornate knobs in aged brass or bronze, but your options are limitless. We recommend avoiding handles or knobs that jut outwards. Living is tight in a van, and you don't want your hardware getting in the way of your movements.

In addition to your standard handle suppliers, Etsy and eBay have some very good options at great prices. Also look at big-box retailers and homewares stores like Anthropologie, and don't discount op shops (thrift stores or charity shops) and antique stores, where you're bound to find the quirkiest options.

MATERIALS TO AVOID:

✶   MDF has terrible properties when it comes to moisture. It's easy to paint and gives a great finish, but the second it gets wet, it will expand and deteriorate.

✶   Avoid loose batt insulation. If this type of insulation gets wet, it will never dry and will go mouldy in the wall.

FLOORING

In our first four vans, we laid timber-look vinyl plank flooring, which we've favoured for its durability and cost. It's easy to install, waterproof and flexible. Interestingly, though, we don't find it easy to clean, which is not ideal for vanning.

In Goldie, we went rogue and laid carpet. It sounds completely nonsensical to lay carpet in a van, but hear us out. We used a product called Tretford carpet, which is most commonly used in high-traffic commercial spaces like offices and shopping centres. It's a durable, sustainable and healthy flooring option, but the key here is that we laid it in 60 × 60cm (23½ × 23½in) tiles. This way, when the sand that will inevitably build up over time does just that, we can pick up the carpet tiles and give them a good shake out. Even better, when the carpet gets stained beyond repair, we can replace only the squares that need replacing.

UPHOLSTERY FABRICS

We've already discussed the power of upholstery and fabrics in introducing colour and pattern in your interior (see page 69), but the functionality of your fabric is of equal importance. Van fabric should be specifically suitable for upholstery, meaning it's of a certain thickness and weight; tested to ensure its efficacy in covering furniture; and suitable for the sort of living that comes with van life. It needs to be able to handle sunscreen, dirty feet and food. Your best bet is to select a fabric that will disguise dirt or to opt for an indoor/outdoor fabric, which is designed to withstand the elements and guaranteed to be easy to clean. We tend to use a mix of outdoor fabric and patterned fabrics for their capacity to hide marks.

Please learn from our mistakes and avoid using velvet in your van. It shows every speck of dust and is not an easy-to-clean option once marked. We would also avoid 100 per cent natural materials like cotton and linen – while they're lovely and breathable, they are subject to fading and typically not as durable as when blended with a synthetic fibre.

PART FOUR

Construction

Vintage vans are old and have often lived hard lives. The trick is to embrace the odd bump and scratch here and there, and accept that even though the overhead cabinets may not be overly practical – with their small openings and awkward layouts – they are a gentle reminder that your van has a history, potentially longer than your own. In the design phase of the renovation, you will have decided what needs to stay and what needs to go. After our first renovation, it dawned on us that for future van renovations we'd need to be more discerning about what *could* be replaced and what *should* be replaced.

DEMOLITION

Don't go in at full speed with a sledgehammer, smashing everything to pieces. It's better to systematically deconstruct the van, taking plenty of photos of the process for future reference. Spend time removing things such as locks, latches, hinges and handles, and if they're in good condition, keep doors and drawers intact. You never know, you might need them later on in the build or you could alter them for another purpose. Most original vans will come with a gas stove that doesn't comply with current regulations and in all cases will need to be removed.

Beyond the beautiful pressed masonite ceiling in Bumblebee, there wasn't much to salvage, but we did pay homage to her vintage origins by hanging the van's original clock in the entry, and it happens to be one of Carlene's favourite features.

With Dolly, we retained as much joinery as we could; however, the ceiling showed signs of water damage around the skylights, so instead of attempting to pull down the entire ceiling without disturbing the cabinets, we opted to batten out the ceiling, insulate, and install VJ panelling. Dolly had her original doorknobs intact, which we spray painted to bring them back to life.

WARNING

Some vintage vans can contain elements of asbestos, and precautions need to be taken during demolition to avoid contact. Asbestos can be found in unexpected locations including, but not limited to, the sealant around the windows, on the backing of vinyl floor tiles and in the brake pads. When it comes to asbestos, leave it undisturbed if possible. If required, there are companies that will test your van for a small fee.

In Vonnie, we salvaged some very sweet original details, like the rounded shelves and metal railing, which we painted. We were even able to retain the original mirror in the overhead cabinet.

With Millie, we basically gutted the interior to have the freedom of a new layout and fresh finishes, but in hindsight, we wish we'd taken a more restorative approach and hadn't been so quick to replace, as it was one of the few vans we secured in good condition. Millie was undoubtedly our guinea pig.

THE TRAILER

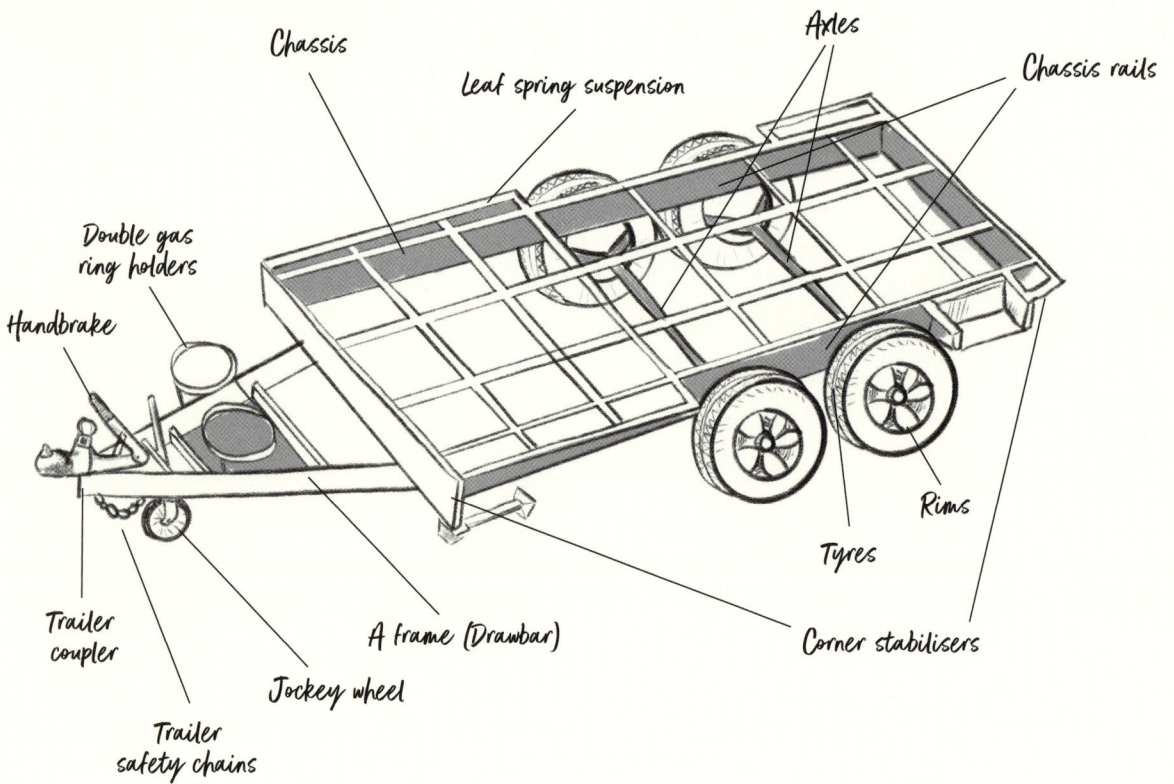

Chassis

Leaf spring suspension

Axles

Chassis rails

Double gas
ring holders

Handbrake

Trailer
coupler

Trailer
safety chains

Jockey wheel

A frame (Drawbar)

Corner stabilisers

Tyres

Rims

WHEELS AND TYRES

Check the tyres. Old tyres can be cracked and worn and close to failing due to years of neglect. Consult your local state and country laws for the legal prerequisites. In Australia, vans require light truck tyres, as opposed to ordinary passenger car tyres.

Make sure to check all the wheel parts to make sure they are in good condition.

WHEEL HUB

Dust caps: Dust caps, also called grease caps, are filled with grease and protect the bearings from dirt, dust, sand, water and the like. Broken or missing dust caps could mean the bearings aren't properly lubricated and could fail and should be replaced before towing. It is also a bad sign if the dust caps get very hot to touch after towing.

Castle nut and split pin: The slotted castle nut, split pin and washer hold the entire hub assembly in place on the axle. The split pin ensures the castle nut doesn't become loose, which would cause the wheel to become loose on the axle. If any of these are missing, the van would be dangerous to tow.

Hub drum: The hub drum assembly consists of the brake drum, the backing plate, the brake pads and the studs and nuts that fasten to the wheels. The backing plate fixes to the axle and remains stationary. The brake pads are fixed to the backing plate.

The drum could be rusted and the brake pads worn beyond their limits or even seized. Never apply grease or lubricant to the brake pads or the drum. This could cause the drum brakes to become inefficient or even fail altogether.

Bearings: The outer and inner bearings, the outer and inner cup and the seal fit inside the hub, which then sits over the spindle. These bearings are packed with grease. Signs that the bearings might fail include evidence of heat (the purpling of the metal) after towing and little or no grease.

parts of a trailer wheel hub

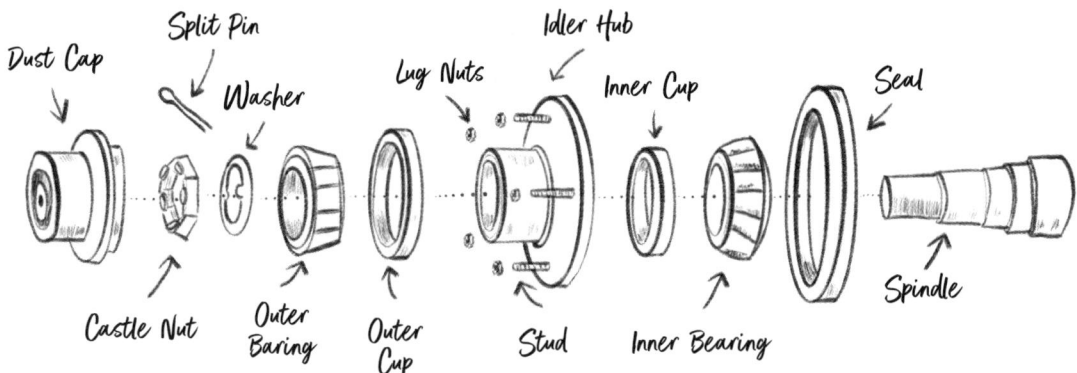

Dust Cap · Split Pin · Washer · Lug Nuts · Idler Hub · Inner Cup · Seal

Castle Nut · Outer Baring · Outer Cup · Stud · Inner Bearing · Spindle

Suspension and axles: These old vans generally have leaf spring suspension, a design which has been around in some form for over 100 years. The left springs are bolted to the chassis through the spring eye and to the axle via the U bolts. This suspension system can be upgraded to take heavier loads. The size of the axle will contribute to determining the total trailer payload (see page 27) and may be upgraded to take larger loads. As long as these components are in good working order, the leaf spring suspension is sufficient for general on-road vanning.

Some van users, particularly those heading off-road, choose to upgrade their suspension to independent trailing arm suspension. Each wheel has its own coil spring and shock absorbers to absorb the bumps. This type of suspension also does away with the cross-vehicle axle, giving the van greater ground clearance for off-road travelling.

Some van users, particularly those heading off-road, choose to upgrade their suspension

WHEEL ARCHES AND FLOORING

During the demolition process, try to preserve the wheel arches and/or take note of their shape and size. A local metal fabricator should be able to create a wheel arch one from galvanised iron sheets to match the existing wheel arches. Some old vans have plastic wheel arches that may have deteriorated or may be missing at the time of purchase. A simple rectangle-shaped wheel arch is all that is required. Be sure to include 2–3cm (0.8–1.2in) tabs that will allow the wheel arch to be fixed to the trailer. The side without the tabs will need to be scribed to the wheel arch of the caravan wall.

RV-specific flooring is available from most timber suppliers. It is constructed from flat, highly water-resistant, lightweight plywood and is covered on one side with a waterproof coating. It is, however, more expensive than ordinary plywood. You can also use 12mm (½in) marine plywood by coating the underside of the sheet with a bitumen waterproofer.

Start by cutting *all* pieces to size and dry-lay them in place without using glue. This will ensure that all the cuts, particularly around the wheel arches, are accurate and will provide a waterproof floor. Once it all fits, apply a bead of polyurethane sealant, such as Sikaflex, to the trailer members and under the metal wheel arches. Secure each floor sheet every 300mm (12in) or so using countersunk, self-tapping metal screws. To fix the wheel arches, screw through the flooring and the metal tabs into the trailer base.

WINDOWS

Old vans typically come with 3–4mm ($\frac{1}{10}$–$\frac{1}{8}$in) float glass windows. This glass is surprisingly heavy and can form dangerously sharp edges if broken. We always replace all original windows with 3mm ($\frac{1}{10}$in) acrylic that you can purchase from a plastic supplier.

The windows have to be pulled out completely by removing the window winders and/or stays and gently, using a mallet and a block of wood, sliding the window sash out. The rubbers can be removed and the top part of the frame unscrewed in the corners and taken out. You should now be able to remove the old glass intact. Take the glass to a plastic supplier, and they'll use it as a template from which to cut the acrylic.

The window frame itself is simply screwed in and can be removed by taking out all the screws and gently prying the frame from the van.

With the window frames disassembled, it's a good opportunity to properly clean them. You'll need a combination of mineral turpentine, a steel wire wheel on a drill, sandpaper and a lot of hard work. Be sure to remove all silicon from the windows as silicon cannot be painted.

The corner windows on a Viscount are a bit more difficult. They require a jig to be made. A jig is a plywood 'pattern' in the same shape as the window that allows the heated acrylic to be bent around it into the correct shape. We get so many questions about these corner windows. It seems every Viscount needs new ones.

To reinstall the acrylic window pane, position the pane in the frame and screw the frame back together. Using a spray bottle with detergent and water, lubricate the new window rubber and begin working it into the frame. Do not try to stretch the rubber, as over time it will begin to pull out of the frame. For 90-degree corners, slice the back of the rubber to help push it right into the corner. Window rubbers can be purchased from most foam and rubber suppliers or vintage caravan retailers.

SEALANTS

Neutral cure silicon

To seal the exterior of the van, we use a neutral cure silicon. Silicon offers a long-lasting, strong and flexible joint. The disadvantage of using silicon is that it's permanent, meaning if you need to remove a window or air conditioner down the track, it could prove difficult without doing some damage. The other problem is that you can't paint silicon. Avoid using acetic cure silicon, as it can cause damage to painted surfaces and soft metals like aluminium.

Neutral cure silicon is recommended for:

* new roof joints

* new or reinstallation of aluminium trims

* window installation

* installing hatches and air conditioners.

Polyurethane

Polyurethane sealants offer a stronger bond than silicon and are popular with van and motorhome builders. Most polyurethane sealants also have the advantage of being able to be sanded and painted and provide more flexibility than silicon. The disadvantage is that they're more expensive, and the strong bond properties will make future works difficult should disassembly be required.

Consider installing an external tap on the drawbar and connect a small hose to it. This hose is very handy for washing feet, surfboards and the like.

PLUMBING

Plumbing is one of those jobs that can be quite easy to carry out yourself and can range from a simple mains pressure system with a hand pump, sink and water tank to an extremely complex system with pumps, hot-water systems, toilets and showers. The system you choose to install in your van will depend on your budget and your requirements.

If you only plan to use your van at caravan parks with a mains water supply, there is no need to allow for pumps and water tanks, saving you money, time and effort. Furthermore, there won't be a need to install toilets and showers if you choose to use parks with amenities.

On the other end of the spectrum, if you plan on leaving the world behind and going off-grid for weeks on end, then your needs will be different. Consider installing more than one water tank, grey-water tanks for sewage water, a hot-water system and a toilet and shower. You can also install an external tap on the drawbar and connect a small hose to it. This hose is very handy for washing feet, surfboards and the like.

The good news is that the plumbing rough-in and fit-off is a relatively simple process, and there are a number of push-fit or screw-on system products on the market that don't need any soldering of copper pipes.

We recommend using John Guest plumbing fittings. These are quick to install, can be undone easily if you make a mistake, are reusable and require no tools for installation.

Only use food-grade hoses and tanks, including the hose that connects the van to the mains water supply, and make sure all the connections remain accessible. Where possible, avoid having connections in the walls. Should any such connections leak down the track, before the leak is recognised they could do untold damage and be costly to rectify.

HAND PUMP

The water tank is installed underneath the van with brackets that are readily available from many plumbing suppliers. A piece of plywood can be included to protect the tank from stone chips, and the tank is filled via a water filler and a food-grade filler hose. Water fillers are relatively cheap and come in many shapes and sizes; they even have lockable caps. The filler hose is usually 25mm (1in) and is fixed to the water tank barb and the water filler with hose clamps.

The hand pump draws water from the tank via 12mm (½in) plumbing pipes and connections. A one-way valve should be installed on the outlet hose near the tank to ensure that the pipes remain primed with water and it doesn't require pumping every time the tap needs to be used.

The drain hose should be a corrugated sewage hose to prevent kinking. A simple method is to connect the sewage hose to the sink drain, and cut it to length so it finishes approximately 100mm (4in) underneath the van. Once the van is set up, a 25mm (1in) barb can be connected, and the additional sewage hose can be joined to the drain and run to the sewer onsite. Alternatively, a 25mm (1in) stopcock together with a 25mm (1in) BSP to barb connector (see illustration above right) can be purchased from most hardware stores. The stopcock can be attached under the van using a bracket in an accessible position.

Simple hand pump plumbing solution

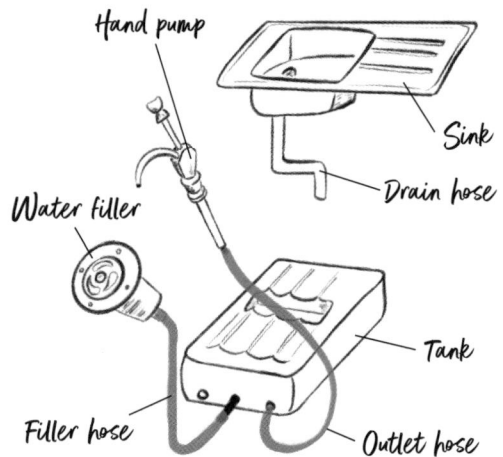

Hand pump · Sink · Drain hose · Water filler · Tank · Filler hose · Outlet hose

ELECTRIC PUMP

The same system can be easily adapted to include an electric pump. Run the plumbing fittings from the water tank through a one-way valve and inline water filter to an electric pump. The one-way valve will ensure the line remains primed. The inline filters normally have a BSP male connector that screws directly into the pump. Ensure that the pump is a 12V pressure pump, as a pressure pump senses the drop in pressure when the tap is opened and starts pumping automatically. If the van has a shower, the pump should be rated for at least 10l (2.64gal) per hour for adequate pressure. The breather hose should be connected to the water filler or positioned to prevent road debris from entering the line. The breather hose allows the water to pump freely.

Electric pump plumbing solution

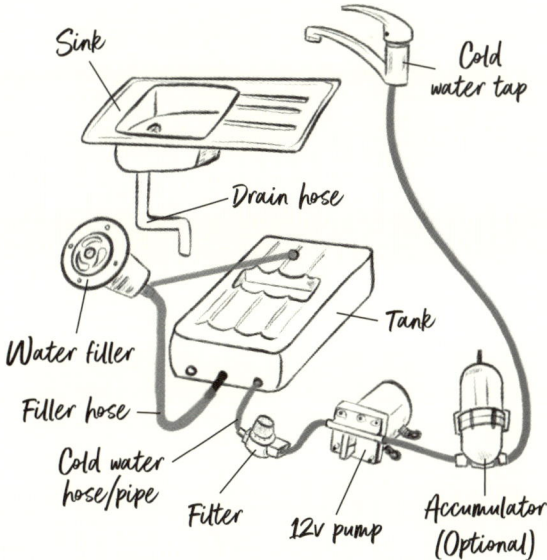

Sink

Cold water tap

Drain hose

Tank

Water filler

Filler hose

Cold water hose/pipe

Filter

12v pump

Accumulator (Optional)

The hot-water heater recovery rate is the amount of hot water that your unit is able to offer in a given period of time, which serves to measure how quickly your hot-water supply is replenished.

For those not setting up their van for off-grid camping, the electric-only model is by far the cheapest and easiest to install. These hot-water systems can fit under a seat or in the back of a cupboard with a door for access from the outside of the van, and have a recovery rate of about 21l (5.53gal) per hour for a 45°C (113°F) rise in temperature.

Gas hot-water systems have either a 12V electric ignition or a manual ignition. Many models offer a separate remote that can be wired to the heater and placed in an accessible position in the van to ignite the system and indicate whether the system is on or off. This type of heater has a 40l (10.55gal) per hour recovery rate for a 45°C (113°F) rise in temperature and a price point in the middle of the range.

An instantaneous hot-water system is the ideal choice for a large family and will provide an endless supply of hot water. The unit will require a 12V power supply for the igniters and a constant gas supply for the burners. The temperatures and different modes can be selected by a control panel. Because these heaters provide constant hot water, there is no recovery rate. This type of hot-water system falls into a high-end price bracket. Some units have integrated pressure-limiting valves and others specify the maximum mains water pressure allowable. Pressure-limiting valves should be installed to ensure no damage to the unit.

MAINS PRESSURE

A pressure-limiting valve may be required to be installed when adding mains pressure to the system, as many hot-water systems have pressure limits. From the pressure-limiting valve, install the water feed pipe to the taps (and hot-water system if installed). If also installing a 12V water pump, a one-way valve can be installed on the outlet pipe of the pump and connected to the main water feed. Note: Either a one-way valve or a stop cock will need to be installed to prevent the water from the pump running out of the mains water inlet if a mains water hose is not connecting.

HOT-WATER SYSTEMS

Hot-water systems for vans range from 240V/110V systems to gas or instantaneous gas hot-water systems. Factors such as the type of application, number of people the system is servicing and recovery rate required will determine the type of hot-water system you need.

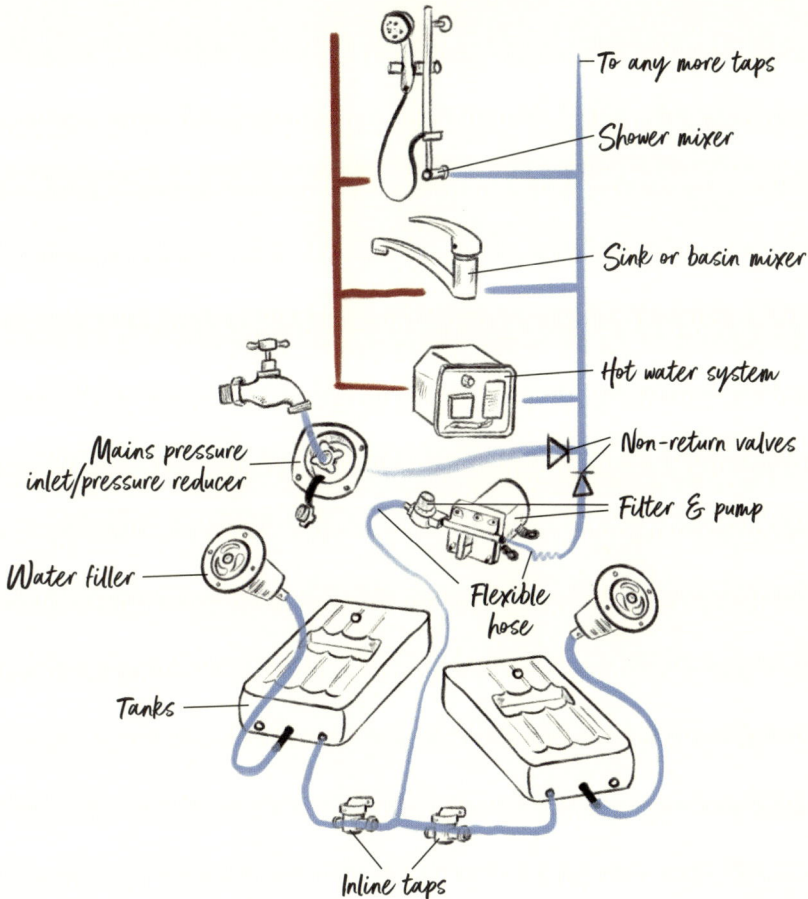

Hot-water systems

To any more taps

Shower mixer

Sink or basin mixer

Hot water system

Non-return valves

Mains pressure inlet/pressure reducer

Filter & pump

Water filler

Flexible hose

Tanks

Inline taps

Always adhere to the installation details. All heaters must be installed on the exterior of the van, as they need to be vented. The vents should be at least 25cm (10in) from any other surface and more than 40cm (16in) from any window or opening into the van. It is important that they are installed on the side opposite to the annex or canopy to prevent venting into an enclosed space.

To connect into the plumbing system, it is advised that the hot-water plumbing is installed using the red tube of the system. The hot-water unit will have a 12 mm (½ in) water outlet that can be connected directly to a brass fitting adapter and to your plumbing system and then run to all the taps in the van. Use pipe-retaining clips to secure pipes and avoid the tap hammering and other vibrations.

Use pipe-retaining clips to secure pipes and avoid the tap hammering and other vibrations.

TAPWARE

You can purchase RV fittings that enable the flexible hose of household taps to be connected to the water supply. These are typically brass with a 12mm (½in) BSP male connection. If hot water is not installed, it's a good idea to split the cold-water supply and connect both the hot and cold flexible hoses to the tap. That way, the tap will work with the mixer in any position.

The gas bottle cannot be installed inside the van and needs a sealed compartment with a vented door accessible from the outside.

GAS

Installing gas pipes and gas appliances is a job for a licensed plumber or gas installer, who is responsible for ensuring the gas installation complies with local regulations and standards. The installer is required to issue a gas/propane certificate before the van can be registered.

Installation

The gas bottle cannot be installed inside the van and needs a sealed box or compartment that has a vented door accessible from the outside. Most vans allow for space on the drawbar to install the gas bottles and regulators, but vans with multiple gas appliances, particularly with instantaneous hot water, opt for two 9kg (20lb) bottles. It is important to ensure that there is no electrical equipment that

could be a source of ignition located near the gas bottles. The gas bottles are connected to a manual valve that allows the user to easily switch between gas bottles (see illustration below left). The valve then feeds a regulator that ensures the outlet gas pressure does not exceed 3 kPa. It is a requirement that the regulators are installed higher than the gas bottle and fitted to a rigid structure, which is often the front panel of the van.

Small to medium-sized vans normally use an 8mm (5⁄16in) copper pipe for the main run from the gas bottles to the appliances, and generally do so underneath the van. Larger vans with multiple gas appliances may use 9mm (3⁄8in) pipe for the main run and branch off into 8mm (5⁄16in) pipe to reach each appliance. As these pipes are susceptible to damage from stone chips and road debris, they need to be protected. You can use poly pipe from the local hardware store that has been split along the length of the pipe and installed and secured in place with saddles over the copper gas line to satisfy this requirement. The saddles should be placed every 60cm (23½in) and have 15cm (6in) on either side of a change in direction to secure the pipes.

Each appliance must have its own branch from the main line into the van. This junction is not permitted to be inside the van or hidden inside walls. The joins must be accessible at all times. Each appliance is also required to have an accessible gas isolation valve, using either a copper pipe or flexible hose – not exceeding 120cm (47in) – to connect the valve to the appliance.

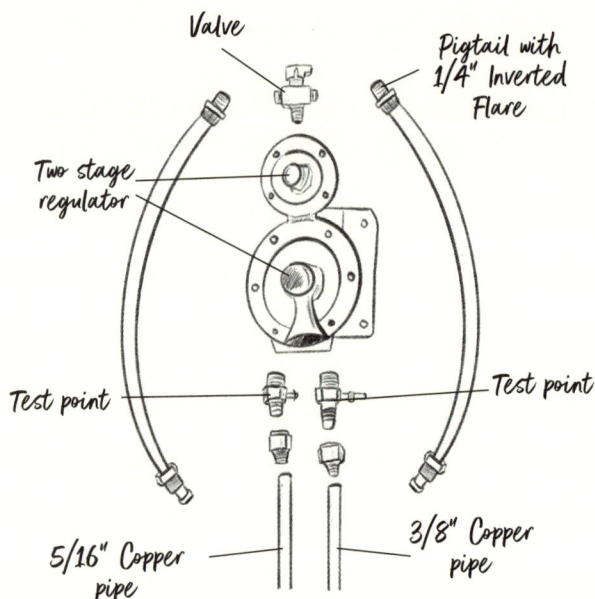

Valve

Pigtail with 1/4" Inverted Flare

Two stage regulator

Test point

Test point

5/16" Copper pipe

3/8" Copper pipe

Ventilation

Gas appliances, such as fridges, heaters and hot-water systems, require venting to outside the van and must operate at or below 2.75kPa. The cabinetry, exhaust and range hoods need to be designed to comply with regulations and standards, often set out in the installation instructions. It's imperative that the flue or exhaust does not vent into an annex or attached enclosure, inlet vents or windows. Portable gas heaters and water heaters without flues aren't allowed to be installed in vans.

While modern appliances such as fridges and hot-water systems are sealed units and vented externally, gas stoves and ovens have the potential to leak gas into the van. Therefore, you must provide permanent and unrestricted ventilation at either end of the van. As gas is heavier than air, vents are required to be installed at both high and low locations. This type of ventilation can be achieved by a combination of vented doors, roof-mounted hatches and floor vents.

Don't forget about the barbecue or grill. A bayonet and quick-connect device can be plumbed into the gas system on the exterior of the van. Like other gas appliances, it needs to be installed outside the annex or any other enclosure.

INTERNAL FIT-OUT

With the electrical and plumbing roughly installed, it's time to complete the internal fit-out. This is where the van starts to somewhat resemble a van.

INSULATION

Whether you are trying to keep the hot air in or out, insulation is essential. To insulate the walls and ceiling, we use a product called foil board, which is polystyrene between two layers of aluminium foil that has excellent thermal and acoustic protection properties. It comes in thicknesses of 10–30mm (⅜–1⅕in) and is a rigid board, meaning it's easy to install. Foil board can be cut with a Stanley knife to make it fit snugly in the wall framing.

Do *not* use the common house-type loose batt insulation. Despite all your efforts, at some point your van may leak. This insulation will become wet and soggy, which is a breeding ground for black mould.

INTERNAL LININGS

Relining a van is a labour-intensive task and requires some carpentry skills to achieve a good finish. If you aren't handy on the tools, consider outsourcing this task to someone who is.

Van manufacturers use a selection of moulds and flexible PVC profiles on the corners of the walls and cabinets, and where they meet the walls and roof. This allows for movement in the cabinetry and walls during travel.

When demolishing the caravan linings, it's a good idea to keep any intact sheets to use as templates. This will save you valuable time and effort.

CEILINGS

Van ceilings can be prone to damage from water leaking through roof sheets, corner trims (J moulds) and skylights. The first step is to fix the leaks. Ceiling sheets can be difficult to replace if the cabinets are to remain, due to how the vans are constructed in the factory. Consider whether it is an easier solution to only replace some parts or to install a new ceiling over the existing one.

If installing a new ceiling, follow the steps below

Step 1
Cut the ceiling sheets to nearly the exact width in between the wall frames. It's important they are not cut too short, as the wall sheet will need to butt into them and cover the edges. Make sure the ceiling sheets are joined on a roof-framing member.

Step 2
Apply a bead of polyurethane sealant, such as Sikaflex, on each roof-framing member.

Step 3
Position a ceiling sheet in place and tack it in position with short T-nails or staples if the roof members are timber or rivets if the members are aluminium. Ensure the sheet is square to the walls. This will be evident by whether the gaps are even or uneven.

Step 4
Continue to nail the sheet at 30cm (12in) intervals.

Step 5
Cut a piece of H-section moulding to run the width of the van and slide it onto the edge of the sheet.

Step 6
Repeat the previous steps until the ceiling is complete. For the roof openings, measure from the previously installed roof sheet.

WALLS

Similar to the ceiling, wall sheets are difficult to replace around cabinetry. In older vans, the walls can be difficult to measure and install due to the curved roofs, the windows and the door openings.

If installing a new ceiling, you can create a template using a sheet of cardboard or corflute (or any scrap lying around) before cutting into expensive wall sheets.

How to install new wall sheets

Step 1
Gradually trim a piece of cardboard or corflute to suit the curved surface and allowing for windows and doors.

Step 2
Transfer the measurements from the template onto the wall sheet and, using a jigsaw or power saw, cut the sheet to size. It's better to leave the sheet slightly larger and make small final adjustments than to cut it too small to start with.

Step 3
Attach an end cap to the top and bottom of the sheet. This cap can be moved slightly up and down to cover the gap between the top and bottom of the wall sheet, the ceiling sheet and the floor. The cap will span over multiple sheets.

Step 4
Apply a bead of polyurethane sealant, such as Sikaflex, on each wall-framing member and attach the wall sheet using rivets or small staples.

Step 5
Attach an H trim to the join of the sheets and continue the process.

UPHOLSTERY

Full disclosure: we've always outsourced our upholstery and reupholstery to a professional, and if your budget allows, we recommend you do the same. When you use a professional upholsterer, you'll not only achieve a professional outcome, but you'll gain access to fabrics that fabric suppliers only supply to trade customers and don't sell directly to the public.

HOW TO UPHOLSTER/REUPHOLSTER

If your budget calls for a DIY job, ensure you have upholstery-weight fabric and use the steps below as a guide.

Items you will need:

* plywood

* scissors and tape measure

* tracing paper if you need to create a new template (you can also use brown paper or even wrapping paper)

* high-density foam

* electric kitchen knife or bread knife

* upholstery-grade polyester batting

* adhesive spray suitable for foam

* staple gun – a powered one is easier to use but a manual gun is fine too.

Step 1

Begin with your base. Plywood is a good, strong base to use and is readily available. Take measurements off the existing seat you wish to replace or create a template using tracing paper. Cut the plywood out yourself or have a timber supplier cut it for you.

Step 2

Most of the time, the foam and batting of the original seat will need replacing. Use good-quality high-density foam from a foam retailer, and consider the finished height of the seat when you select the thickness of the foam – the thicker the foam, the higher your seat will be. Cut the foam to the same shape as the base. If you don't have a foam cutter, an electric kitchen knife or even a bread knife will do the trick. Some foam retailers will cut the foam to size for you.

Step 3

Once the foam is cut to size, place it on the plywood backing and lay a piece of batting the same size as the foam over the top. Glue the batting to the foam with an adhesive spray suitable for foam.

Step 4

Wrap another layer of batting around the entire foam block and staple it to the base of the plywood. This will soften the edges of the plywood base. Start in the middle of each side and then work along to the corners. Work on opposite sides as you go around and try not to pull too tight in any direction, as this will warp the shape of the foam. Pleat around the corners for a softer, rounded look, or fold and tuck the excess batting under for a more square, streamlined look. Place the staples 2.5cm (1in) or so apart, and trim off any excess batting.

Make sure any pattern or grain is running in the right direction before you staple the fabric!

Step 5

Lay the fabric out right side down on your workspace, and centre the batting-wrapped foam block on the fabric with the plywood base facing up. Make sure there is enough fabric to cover all sides with at least 5cm (2in) excess. Like with the batting, start in the middle of each side and and work on opposite sides as you go around to reach each corners. Staple the fabric to the backing board, keeping it snug but not pulling it too tight. Make sure any pattern or grain is running in the right direction before you staple the fabric!

Step 6

Glue the upholstered block back onto the base with strong liquid glue.

Painting & decals

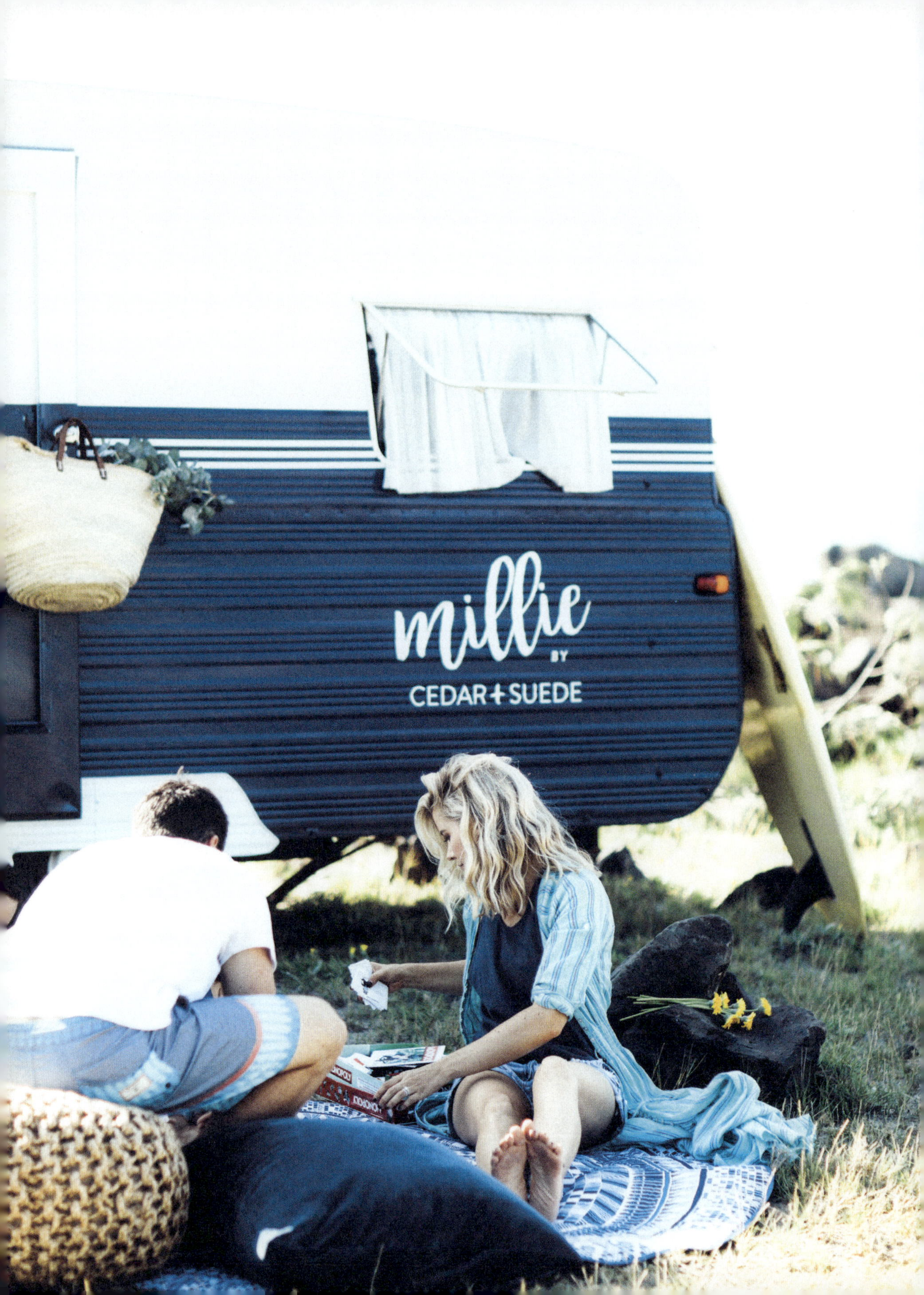
millie
BY
CEDAR + SUEDE

PAINTING THE EXTERIOR

THE CHASSIS

The extent of your renovation will determine how you approach the remedial work and repainting of the trailer chassis. If you are conducting a superficial renovation, then be prepared for a lot of time working under the caravan (yuck). However, if you are completely stripping back the van, like in Goldie's case, this can make life a little easier. Although it might sound daunting, it's actually not a huge task to remove the trailer chassis from the framework of the van. In Goldie, it was a matter of removing eight bolts, and we then were able to get the chassis professionally sandblasted. This gives you full access to the trailer and any otherwise concealed problem areas.

Painting the chassis can be broken down into three processes removing loose rust, treating remaining rust and painting. We make it a little easier by parking the van on some ramps, which gives us an extra 30cm (12in) of room while working underneath. Take extreme care when working under a van that is up on jacks or ramps, and stack piles of timber under the axle in case a jack or ramp gives way or the van rolls off.

Removing rust

Use a wire brush on a drill and remove any loose surface rust, which will almost certainly be present. It's not a fun job. It's a step that we dread.

For any serious rust, we recommend the trailer be inspected by a metal fabricator to determine if any structural damage has occurred and how it can be repaired. It's not uncommon for these vintage vans to require complete drawbar replacement, which is not cheap.

Treating rust

Clean the chassis with a solvent suitable for cleaning metal and treat rusted areas with a rust inhibitor to prevent further corrosion and to prepare the chassis for priming.

Painting

Prime the chassis using a metal etch primer. The etch primer will provide an excellent base for the topcoat and has anti-corrosive properties. It can be sprayed, rolled or brushed on. We've found the easiest and quickest method is to use a small handheld spray gun. They are relatively inexpensive to purchase and easy to operate and clean.

Finish by applying two coats of an exterior metal paint. Like the primer, the topcoat can be sprayed, rolled or brushed on. A hammer tone finish will help hide any stone chips and dirt that your van is likely to encounter. Using a dark colour will ensure the chassis doesn't stand out against your van exterior.

Personal protective equipment is a must during this process. This includes earmuffs, eye protection, a mask, a long-sleeved shirt and pants.

PAINTING THE CLADDING

Painting your van exterior is arguably the most transformative component of the renovation and has the power to turn your dilapidated van into something truly special. You will have already selected the colour in the design phase of the process.

There are a couple of ways you can approach the painting of your van's cladding. Hands down the most cost-effective approach is to paint it yourself, but for the most professional, hard-wearing result – and in particular if your van's panelling is pretty banged up– hand it over to the experts and let an automotive painter do the job.

Automotive painting

Most autobody shops, panel beaters and smash repair services will have the capacity to paint your van. It's just a matter of whether they want to or not. Not all automotive painters will want the job, because vans offer some challenges that cars don't, which is why it's never a cheap job. We've paid AU$4500–AU$7000 (US$3500–US$5500), which included patching dings.

Your old van is bound to have some small dints in the panelling which we embrace as part of the character, but if it's substantially banged-up, you'll need to have your automotive painter patch at least the major ones. Addressing all of the imperfections is labour intensive and might be cost prohibitive. Rest assured though that a professional paint job is significantly more effective at disguising dints than DIY paint.

You'll require approximately 1l (34 fl oz) of paint for 12-14m² (130-150sq ft) of surface coverage, which will give you two coats of paint, but we recommend having your paint supplier work out your quantity based on how you intend to apply it (that is, brush, roller, spray gun or all of the above).

DIY painting

If you're taking the DIY approach to painting, you're going to save yourself a few thousand dollars, but be mindful, as even the best painter can't achieve the same result as an auto painter. You won't be able to achieve that hardy gloss finish that you see on car surfaces either.

As with any painting project, preparation is key. Start by removing all exterior fittings, including lights, reflectors, doors, windows, power inlets, wheel spats, etc. These old vans can have up to 60 years of silicon on the exterior from previous owners attempting to patch leaks over the years. The bad news is that every bit of this silicon must be removed. You can't paint silicon, and you'll end up with a substandard finish if you attempt to paint over it. You'll also probably find all sorts of waterproofing membranes have been applied to the roof of your van. These too will need to be removed, using a combination of a wire brush on a drill, scrapers and an orbital sander. Also, remove any old flaking paint and other imperfections on the surface.

Rectifying imperfections on the body work can be difficult, as the panels generally have a profile on them. Small dints and holes can be patched using an auto filler, and any large holes may require the full sheet to be replaced. It's not an easy task, and that's if you can even find the correct sheet profile. It's the reason why substantial damage on the cladding is a red flag to us during the pre-purchase inspection. Afterwards, give the surface a good clean using a solvent suitable for metal cleaning. This will remove any dirt, dust and grease before priming.

Using painters tape and masking paper or plastic film, tape up any areas that aren't to be painted (that is, the windows). Using an etch primer, prime the surface by spraying, rolling or brushing it on.

To achieve a two-tone paint scheme, start with painting the topcoat of the lighter colour first. Following the paint manufacturer's instructions, apply at least two coats of topcoat. We use a water-based metal enamel paint. Be sure to paint well past the section where you wish to join the two paint colours.

Once dry, mask up the lighter colour. Run a line of painters tape to define the junction between the two colours. Take your time with this step, as it will be very noticeable if the line isn't straight. Stand close to the van and look down the line to make adjustments.

To achieve a nice clean line, apply the second coat and remove the tape before it dries. Note: Do not leave the painters tape on the van for extended periods or it will become difficult to remove and may even take the paint off with it.

PAINTING THE INTERIOR

If the cabinets are largely intact, the right colour and type of paint can be enough to take these surfaces from drab to fab.

PAINTING LAMINATE

In these old vans, not only is the cabinetry typically covered in a laminate surface but commonly the walls are too. Don't be fooled by their dreary appearance. If the cabinets are largely intact, the right colour and type of paint can be enough to take these surfaces from drab to fab.

Laminate paint is typically our go-to when it comes to painting the interiors. It's hard wearing, easy to clean, and can be applied by either brush, roller or spray gun.

Because the original cabinetry is usually a gloss laminate finish, it will require some preparation to make the paint stick. Remove all cabinet doors and drawers, and all hinges, locks, handles, drawer runners, etc. Give the surface a good sand with an orbital sander and fix any imperfections. For large holes and dints, use a two-part builders bog. For any small imperfections use a lightweight, fast-drying, non-shrinking filler and fill any small gaps with a multipurpose, water-based gap filler.

Use a specific laminate surface cleaner to remove dust and grease, and prime the surface using a tile and laminate primer. This is important. If it's not done correctly, the paint won't adhere to the surface and will peel off in sheets.

Allow the primer to dry and apply the first coat of the laminate paint. This paint can be tinted to any colour. Allow it to dry and give the surface a light sand. This will remove any high spots in the paint.

Finally, apply the second coat and stand back to admire the transformation.

SPRAY PAINTING SMALL METALS

We use a good-quality acrylic enamel spray paint and primer in one to paint any existing metals in the van interior. In nearly all our vans, we've used satin gold spray paint in some capacity. In Dolly, we used it to paint things like the legs of the original dining table, as well as the original metal fretwork that supports the shelves. In Bumblebee, we used it to paint the original table-edge trim.

What you will need:

* good-quality acrylic enamel spray paint

* 400 grit sandpaper

* drop sheets

* dust mask

* clean rags.

Step 1

To achieve a high-quality finish, preparation is key. Make sure your surface is clean, dry and free from dust, dirt, grease and other contaminants.

Step 2

Sand previously painted or glossy surfaces with 400 grit sandpaper.

Step 3

Give the spray can a good shake for about a minute after the ball inside starts to rattle. Then, hold it upright and spray in a sweeping motion about 15–20cm (6–8in) away from the surface.

We spray painted the leg of the original dining table.

THE DECAL

The first thing you need to know is that decals are created by a sign writer. It's the simplest, most non-fuss part of the whole renovation process, yet it has so much impact. We use a website called DaFont.com, which offers thousands of free downloadable fonts. Type your van name in the tab provided, and you'll be shown what your name will look like in your selected font. There is no right or wrong. Simply find a font that feels right for your scheme.

We send the text and font to a sign writer, along with an image of the van and the dimensions of our desired stripe. The sign writer superimposes the decal onto an image of the van, so that we can propose adjustments before signing off. Consider the scale of your decal in proportion to the van. Personally, we want to make sure the stripes are the right distance apart and sitting at the desired height on the van. From there, the sign writer will simply print the decal and will need approximately 1–2 hours for installation.

millie

BY

CEDAR+SUEDE

PART SIX

Decoration

Unlike our home interiors, a van is the one place that we like to keep small decor and loose furnishings to an absolute minimum. Small-space living is not the time to get creative with styling your horizontal surfaces. In fact, we like to keep our horizontal surfaces clear to reduce visual chaos and to ensure we are living in the van with ease. If you're partial to a layered space, utilise your vertical surfaces to add interest – just make sure, you're adding things like art and clocks, that they are installed very securely so they will survive travel.

WINDOW FURNISHINGS

Carlene has conflicting feelings about the window furnishings in our vans. She *loves* the look of simple sheer curtains – they're visually light, which is ideal for a small space, and through the day they diffuse light and provide some privacy. However, their effectiveness as a window covering stops there. A sheer fabric doesn't stand a chance against that blinding morning sun that comes in hard and strong from 4.30am in the summer, and no one wants their kids waking up with the sun, because we all know how that turns out!

The first step in determining your window coverings is to work out your light and privacy requirements, and this will vary depending on the people occupying the space. For example, those who don't mind waking up with the sun have no reason to include blockout curtains, which is an opportunity to save on both fabric cost and labour, but those who need full darkness to sleep will require a full blockout option.

Depending on your light and privacy needs, you could also consider blinds. Horizontal blinds, roman blinds and roller blinds could all work if you were willing to have them made to fit a van window (see the illustrations below). Personally, we'll always favour what curtains bring to a space, like softness, femininity and ease, and in Goldie's case, an opportunity to inject some fun (see page 181).

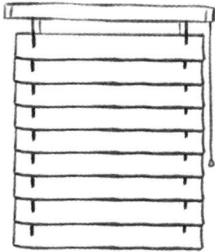

Horizontal blinds

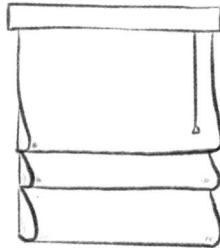

Roman blinds

Roller blinds

The range of options available in curtains is vast. Mounting options include rods or tracks with rings, clips, glides and more. Curtain heading options include gathered, pencil pleat, box pleat and pinch pleat – the list goes on and on, and it's enough to make your head spin!

Note: We don't recommend using pinch pleat curtains, as they require too much fabric and add unnecessary bulk to a small space like a van. We've looked at lots of different options with thought to all the considerations unique to van windows and van life, and we've found that a combination of blockout and sheer, gathered curtains on a mini track provides us the best solution.

For all our vans, we've engaged a local sewer, rather than a specialised curtain manufacturer. If you're lucky, your local sewer might be a friend or family member, or you might even have managed to retain some high school sewing skills yourself. Even those of us without any sewing abilities can still make our own curtains, thanks to iron-on tape and clip-on hooks, but sewing will open you up to more choice in curtain styles.

For Millie, Vonnie and Bumblebee, we went with simple sheer cafe curtains gathered on caravan cord. You can purchase cord and hooks from Ebay.

For heavier fabrics like linens and blockout fabrics, the curtains require a track to move easily and freely. This was the case for Goldie. From a caravan and motorhome supply company online , we sourced a bendable mini curtain track that could be either wall or ceiling mounted.

MEASURING UP FOR YOUR CURTAINS

* Take the measurement from where the hooks will sit on the track or rod, not just the window opening sizes. Allow for extra fabric at the top to create the heading, which will cover the track.

* Think about furniture and joinery that might sit below the curtains, such as a banquette back rest, and allow for enough clearance to pull the curtain across.

* Allow for enough clearance over countertops for items such as cutting boards, appliances and power points.

* Allow some space at the sides of the windows for the curtain to be pulled back – this is called stack back. The less stack back you have, the more the curtain will cover the window, even when pulled back.

* Think about how the curtain will open, and consider doing single-panel curtains that can be pulled either way, rather than two panels with a centre opening, as this can be restrictive.

* When measuring up for a blockout curtain, make the curtain size bigger than the window opening to eliminate light leaking through the gaps.

* Vans typically have a lot of small-scale windows, so try to be consistent in aligning tops and bottoms of curtains throughout the van where possible to reduce visual busyness.

When shopping for fabric, don't limit yourself to just 'curtain or upholstery' fabrics. The small scale of van windows means you're not limited to the wide width, making dress fabrics an option as well. You'll find plenty of interesting possibilities if you look outside the box.

BUYING CURTAIN FABRICS

* Decide on the curtain style and mounting type.

* Measure the window opening and track or pole length.

* Calculate the fabric measurements based on fullness required and your desired drop length. Curtain fullness is the amount of fabric you use within the length of the curtain track (the width of the window). As a general rule, pencil pleat requires fabric twice the length of the track, and sheer cafe curtains two to three times the length.

* Once you've calculated the width measurement based on your desired curtain style, multiply this measurement by the length of your curtains. Add in seam allowances for all the measurements, plus hem and header allowance. This will give you the quantity of fabric to purchase.

In Goldie, we took our use of curtains to the next level, and instead of using them merely in a functional capacity, we made sure they were designed as part of the van's overall aesthetic. In fact, you could say they were central to the success of the interior scheme. However, departing from our usual, simple sheer curtains did come with many more considerations.

Blockout fabric is thicker and heavier than sheer fabric, and therefore doesn't fall in the same relaxed, flowy way that we like. Blockout fabric also adds more bulk to a space, which is emphasised even more when used in a short drop, as is the case with van windows. We therefore wanted to limit our use of blockout fabric where possible, while still ensuring that we weren't impacted by unwanted light while sleeping.

In Goldie, we used internal curtains to create sleeping zones, which allowed us to avoid having to use blockout curtains on all the windows. This way, we only required blockout curtains for the queen-size bed and bunk windows, which meant we could keep to just sheer curtains over our bench seat area.

FREE-STANDING FURNITURE

As in any small-space decor, free-standing furniture in a van should be kept to an absolute minimum, and anything you want to include needs to be able to be stored securely when travelling. For vanning, 99.9 per cent of your furniture should be built in for easy travel.

Vonnie's original layout included a sweet nook that could really be used for whatever we wanted it to be used for. The space was calling for a lightweight stool, and we found a very uncool old stool at our local tip that we upcycled by spray painting the frame and covering the cushion top with leftover fabric from another project. It only works here because the frame is slim and made from super lightweight aluminium that can be moved around with ease.

BED LINENS

Your bedding requirements are going to be subject to the climate at your vanning destination, but given the tight living conditions of a van, excess of anything, including bedding, is just a hindrance. In Dolly, we initially used a quilt like we use at home, but we were always trying to kick it off, and in a van there's nowhere for it to go. We replaced it with a bedspread, which is less bulky, can be tucked in and, generally, takes up less room.

Carlene knows how much people love white, but she recommends avoiding solid white bed sheets in a van. It's not because she thinks white in a van is a

missed opportunity (she does), but from a practical standpoint, it's just not going to withstand those caravan park feet that inevitably make their way onto the white surfaces. And if you're like us, you don't want to have to be precious in your space, especially when you're holidaying.

The kids' bedding also offers an excellent opportunity to add some playfulness to the space in a non-permanent capacity via a combination of contrasting patterns. In Goldie, the classic stripe quilt cover pairs with a floral sheet set for some mix-n-match fun (see page 107).

THROW CUSHIONS

When it comes to our vans, Carlene's a maximalist with colour but minimalist everywhere else. Living in a small space, it's important to us that we do everything we can to ensure we're living in our space together comfortably, and that means not travelling with anything that doesn't serve a purpose. Anything loose like a cushion will inevitably make its way to the floor (kids *love* throwing cushions on the floor), and in a tight space like a van, it will only create a trip hazard. We recommend keeping loose cushions to a minimum and letting your built-in upholstery do its job. If you do want to include throw cushions, as you did with your upholstery, make sure to select a fabric that can withstand camp life. Carlene also recommends having a dedicated space to store them for when you want them out of the way.

RUGS

Rugs are something Carlene can totally get on board with in the context of a van. We're yet to include one in any of our vans, but she loves the idea of a runner-style rug that could also qualify as a mat to wipe your feet on before jumping into bed. There are even machine-washable rugs out there that could service this very purpose. Look for something highly patterned that appears as though it can bear the brunt of grubby camping feet. If you do choose to include a rug, Carlene recommends using a rug underlay to prevent it from slipping around. We typically find the things that you can tolerate in a house are less tolerable in small-space living, and an askew rug is one of those things.

MIRRORS

Most of our vintage vans have come with a mirror of some kind, and for some reason they're always in pretty good condition despite their age. If you need to demolish the surface the mirror is mounted on, you have no choice but to discard it, but try to retain it if you can.

If your van doesn't come with a mirror, it's a good idea to add one somewhere, and adding it to a wardrobe front makes sense. Apart from the obvious benefit of being able to see your reflection when you need to, mirrors are effective at bouncing light around and creating the illusion of space, which is always a good thing in small spaces. Consider a frameless mirror in order to keep the weight down.

In Dolly we retained the original mirror

In Goldie, there was no mirror to salvage. Carlene's plan was to install a mirror on the door front of the free-standing wardrobe, but the vacant space above the drawers was screaming for a mirror, and we already had a sweet art deco mirror in our house that needed a purpose. It was ideal for this space so there was no point in arguing the obvious.

BASKETS

Baskets in hard and soft form will provide infinite opportunities in a van. We use hard baskets in cupboards to store things like medicines, clothing and even food. Anything you can get off your horizontal surfaces will also make your small-space living more functional and clutter-free. Think of all the things that end up scattered across your flat surfaces (for us it's always hats, keys and sunglasses) and make a basket just for them.

Even if your family don't always put their things where they should, baskets serve as designated spots for easy clean up, and you'll all know where to look when your kids inevitably ask. Baskets can also be hung from hooks and can house things like family toiletries, so that they are contained and easily accessible for the trips to the caravan park bathroom.

With each van, Carlene carries out an 'orientation' with the family, so that everyone knows where everything is located and to avoid the 'where is this, where is that?' questions.

HOOKS

You almost can't have too many hooks in a van. They are incredibly handy at keeping your space organised and reducing small-space chaos. Carlene likes to include hooks large enough to hold things like hats and bathrobes, as well as smaller hooks to keep keys and sunglasses by the entry.

You can purchase hooks very affordably at just about any hardware store, but we've found online retailers like eBay and Etsy have a good range at good prices. When choosing your hooks, consider your other metal choices (for more information see page 59) or feel free to mix things up.

BOOKSHELVES

You can expect unwelcome obstacles along your van renovation journey, but you'll also have some pleasant surprises. In more than one of our vans, we've stumbled across opportunities for bookshelves that weren't necessarily part of the initial plan.

In Goldie, we included a combination of simple aged brass hooks and clean, contemporary timber hooks. We also took the opportunity to make the lip of the bookshelf high enough that the books don't need to come out for travel.

PHILIPPA GREGORY
MATTHEW REILLY
jojo moyes
JODI PICOULT
JAMES ROLLINS
DAVID McCULLOUGH
THE WRIGHT BROTHERS
RICHARD BRANSON
a fortunate life

KITCHENWARES

Now, you might deem this a bit pretentious, but Carlene selects kitchen items in accordance with our van's interior colour scheme. This includes things like water glasses, mugs, plates and tea towels. Small spaces like vans just aren't able to swallow up eclecticism like a house interior can, unless of course eclectic is your scheme from the get-go and you've made choices to achieve this along the way. It's a look in its own right that Carlene typically employs for our home interior, but in the small space of our vans, she likes to keep it fairly uniform.

In the small space of our vans, we like to keep kitchenwares fairly uniform.

Vonnie

Appendix

SHOPPING GUIDE

To save you disappearing down the rabbit hole that is sourcing/shopping for everything that comes with these renovations, we've included a helpful list of almost everything used in our vans including where we purchased it. These are specific products we purchased from suppliers and stores in Australia, but you can search online and in your local stores to find similar items wherever you live.

VAN NO. 1 – MILLIE

EXTERIOR

* Exterior paint:
    * Top colour: a white 2pac selected from the Automotive Painters chart but a good white is Dulux Taubmans Big White.
    * Bottom colour: A navy blue 2pac selected from the Automotive Painters chart but a good navy is Dulux Coast
* Decal sign: Designed by us and made and installed by Advanced Signworks

INTERIOR

General finishes

* Paint colour: (light blue): Low sheen enamel paint in Resene Botticelli
* Flooring: Godfrey Hirst, Spotted Gum vinyl plank flooring from DecoRug
* VJ cabinetry (kitchen, overhead cabinets and wardrobe: IKEA
* Handles: Brass shell handles, IKEA
* VJ panelled ceiling - custom made by Wilson Timbers
* Curtains: Montpellier in colour Snow, from Warwick Fabrics

Dining

* Table tiles: Penny round ceramic tiles in gloss, National Tiles
* Table frame: original table, painted in White Knight Squirts in Satin Gold
* Pendant light: Rattan round pendant, Wisteria Design

* Bench seat:
    * Foam and sewing by Foamworld, Burleigh
    * Bench fabric (backrest): Jigsaw in Indigo from Warwick Fabrics
    * Bench fabric (seat): Noosa outdoor fabric in Navy from Warwick Fabrics

Kitchen

* Oak veneer benchtop: IKEA
* Splashback: Carrara marble subway tiles, National Tiles
* Tap: IKEA
* Sink: Stainless steel round sink with chopping board insert, Ebay

Beds

* Paint colour: Resene Prussian Blue in semi-gloss
* Queen bed quilt cover: Lorraine Lea
* Blue Throw Blanket: Kira and Kira
* Cushion: Citta Design
* Kids bed bedpolka dot fitted bed sheets: Cotton On Kids
* Kids bed striped quilt covers and pillowcases: Linen House
* Bedside wall light: IKEA

VAN NO. 2 – VONNIE

EXTERIOR

* Paint:

    * Top colour: White Knight Rust Guard tinted in Taubmans Big White

    * Bottom colour: White Knight Rust Guard tinted in Taubmans Sussex

* Decal: Designed by us and made and installed by Advanced Signworks

* Roof hatch: Camec

INTERIOR
General finishes

* Paint: White Knight Tile and Laminate Paint tinted in Taubmans Sussex and Taubmans Big White

* Flooring: Godfrey Hirst "Spotted Gum" vinyl plank flooring from DecoRug

* Cabinetry/joinery: Original, painted in White Knight Tile and Laminate Paint in colour, Taubmans Sussex

* Cabinet Knobs: Lister knob from Kethy

* Ceiling: VJ plywood panelling custom made by local timber supplier, Wilson Timbers

* Roof hatch: Camec

* Curtains:

    * Fabric: Montpellier in Snow, Warwick Fabrics and made by a local sewer.

    * Caravan cord and hooks: Ebay

* Clock: Original

Dining

* Bench seat:

    * Foam and sewing by Foamworld, Burleigh

    * Bench fabric (backrest): Alanis Forest from Warwick Fabrics

    * Bench fabric (seat): Liaison New Forest from Warwick Fabrics

    * Dining tabletop: Carrara Marble Mosaic tile from National Tiles

    * Brass edging: George White and Co.

    * Base: Original spray painted in White Knight Squirts in Satin Gold

Kitchen

* Kitchen benchtop: "Carrara marble" laminate by Laminex

* Kitchen splashback: Tic Tac Tiles 3D Peel and Stick Wall Tile Subway White, Ebay

* Refrigerator: Dometic CoolMatic 140L Caravan RV Motorhome Refrigerator Fridge Freezer.

* Kitchen tapware: direct import

* Kitchen stovetop: Camec

* Kitchen sink: Ebay

Queen bed

* Quilt cover and Pillowcases: Linen House

Nook

* Stool: An upcycled opp shop/thrift store purchase.

    * Frame: painted in White Knight Squirts Satin Gold

    * Seat: covered in the Grasstree Rust fabric by These Walls.

* Benchtop: Godfrey Hirst "Spotted Gum" vinyl plank flooring from DecoRug

* Wall light: Norwest wall light in brass, Beacon Lighting

VAN NO. 3 – DOLLY

EXTERIOR

- Paint: 2pac paint by Automotive painter in the below colours:
  - Top colour: Taubmans Big White
  - Bottom colour: Taubmans Crashing Waves
- Decal: designed by us and made and installed by Advanced Signworks

INTERIOR

General finishes

- Interior paint:
  - Powder Blue: White Knight Tile and Laminate paint in Taubmans Crashing Waves
  - White: Taubmans Big White
- Flooring: Godfrey Hirst "Spotted Gum" vinyl planks from DecoRug
- Cabinetry/joinery: Original cabinetry painted in White Knight Laminate Paint tinted in Taubmans Crashing Waves
- Cabinetry brass mesh inserts: brass mesh sourced from Arrow Metal
- Cabinetry knobs: Original knobs, painted in White Knight Squirts in Satin Gold
- Curtains
  - Fabric: Warwick Fabric
  - Caravan cord and hooks: Ebay

Dining

- Bench seat:
  - Original foam. Sewing by Foamworld, Burleigh
  - Bench fabric backrest: Palm Paisley in Sapphire from 3Beaches
  - Bench fabric seat: Navy Velvet from Warwick Fabrics
- Dining table: Original tabletop, resurfaced in Carrara Laminate from Laminex
- Brass edging: George White and Co.

Kitchen

- Kitchen benchtop: Carrara marble diamond gloss laminate from Laminex
- Kitchen splashback: Tic Tac Tiles 3D Peel and Stick Wall Tile Subway White, Ebay
- Kitchen tapware: Imported direct (Cedar and Suede)
- Refrigerator: Dometic CoolMatic 140L Caravan RV Motorhome Refrigerator Fridge Freezer.
- Kitchen sink: round 450mm stainless steel sink from Camec

Queen Bed

- Queen bed quilt cover: Adairs

Bunk beds

- Quilt covers from Linen House
- Sheets from Savannah and Three
- Pillowcases from Pottery Barn Kids
- Bed ladder: Custom made by Michael using dowel timber and brass plumbing parts

VAN NO. 4 – BUMBLEBEE AKA BB

EXTERIOR

- Paint: 2pac paint by Automotive painter in the below colours:
  - Top colour: Taubmans Big White
  - Bottom colour: Taubmans Sundial
- Decal: designed by us and made and installed by Advanced Signworks

INTERIOR

General finishes

- Interior paint (white): Taubmans Big White in low sheen
- Flooring: Godfrey Hirst 'Spotted Gum' vinyl plank flooring from DecoRug
- Rattan cabinetry: IKEA oak timber doors modified with rattan insert (you can now
- purchase oak and rattan doors from IKEA
- Cabinet knobs: Kethy
- Curtains:
  - Fabric: Montpellier Snow from Warwick Fabrics
  - Caravan cord and hooks: Ebay
- Clock: Original

Dining

- Dining table: Resurfaced in Carrara Marble Laminate from Laminex
- Bench seat:
  - foam and sewing by Foamworld, Burleigh
  - Bench fabric (back rest): Hattie Daffodil from Warwick Fabrics
  - Bench fabric (seat): Ambrosia Daffodil from Warwick Fabrics
- Pendant light: Byron Pendant from Beacon Lighting

Kitchen

- Benchtop: Carrara Marble Laminate from Laminex
- Kitchen tapware: Direct import (Cedar and Suede)
- Stove: Dometic
- Refrigerator: Dometic CoolMatic 140L Caravan RV Motorhome Refrigerator Fridge Freezer.
- Sink: Round stainless-steel sink, Ebay

Bed

- Quilt cover: Linen House
- Pillowcases: Adairs
- Cushions: Adairs

VAN NO. 5 – GOLDIE

EXTERIOR

* Paint: 2pac paint by Automotive painter:
  * Top colour: Taubmans Coloursmith Peachy Keen
  * Bottom colour: Taubmans Coloursmith Berry Good
* Decal: designed by us and made and installed by Advanced Signworks
* Roof hatch: Ebay
* Wall light: Emac and Lawton

Kitchen

* Tabletop: Catalana marble Natural laminate from Laminex
* Table edging: ABS edging in Kalamata Flint from Laminex
* Handles: Yester Home UK from Etsy
* Tap: Mixer Faucet with Long Reach Spout in chrome from The Boat Warehouse
* Sink: Satinless Steel round basin and drainer from Camec
* Stove: Single Electric Stove from Road Tech Marine

INTERIOR
General finishes

* Wall panelling: Bracing plywood, sealed in a clear polyurethane.
* Interior paint colours: Taubmans Coloursmith Rouge
* Wall lights: Emac and Lawton
* Handles: Yester Home UK from Etsy
* Carpet: Tretford Carpets in mushroom from Gibbon Group

Curtains

* Fabrics: Warwick Fabrics and Walter G

Bench seat

* Foam and sewing by Foamworld, Burleigh
* Bench fabrics from Warwick Fabrics
* Throw cushions: Pahari Saffron linen cushion, Walter G

Café table

* Tabletop: "Catalana marble Natural" laminate from Laminex
* Table edging: ABS edging in "Kalamata Flint" from Laminex
* Pedestal table base: "Tivoli" pedestal base from Temple and Webster

All bedding including sheets and quilt covers:
* Adairs

Wardrobe space

* Wardrobe: Vintage from Facebook Marketplace
* Mirror: Vintage from our own collection
* Basket (inside wardrobe): Bolga basket from Bashiri
* Small décor (vase and bowl) Dinosaur Designs

INDEX

PHOTO CREDITS

VAN PHOTOGRAPHY

* Millie images – Carly Brown
* Vonnie images – Mindi Cooke
* Dolly images – Cait Miers
* Bumblebee images – Cait Miers
* Goldie images (interior) Mindi Cooke
* Goldie images (exterior) Ben Adams

FABRIC PATTERNS

* Pages 22–25 Lanark Colour Cardinal by James Dunlop Textiles
* Pages 70–71 Lanark colour Duck Egg by James Dunlop Textiles
* Pages 108–109 Lanark colour Slate by James Dunlop Textiles
* Pages 48, 61 Grasstree Rust by These Walls
* Pages 50, 68, 80, 185, 189 Bibury by Warwick Fabrics
* Pages 36, 76, 188 Cadiz Riviera Linen – Walter G
* Pages 175, 182 Cadiz Emerald Linen– Walter G
* Pages 50, 51, 85, 190 Pahari Saffron Linen – Walter G
* Pages 63, 67, 129, 178, 209 Lyon Saffron Linen – Walter G
* Pages 17, 43, 130 Corfu Azure Linen – Walter G
* Pages 38, 82, 183 Marabella Saffron Linen – Walter G
* Page 88 Zanzibar Azure Linen – Walter G
* Page 159 Amulet Azure Linen – Walter G

Published in 2023 by Hardie Grant Explore,
an imprint of Hardie Grant Publishing

Hardie Grant Explore (Melbourne)
Wurundjeri Country
Building 1, 658 Church Street
Richmond, Victoria 3121

Hardie Grant Explore (Sydney)
Gadigal Country
Level 7, 45 Jones Street
Ultimo, NSW 2007

www.hardiegrant.com/au/explore

A catalogue record for this
book is available from the
National Library of Australia

NATIONAL
LIBRARY
OF AUSTRALIA

Hardie Grant acknowledges the Traditional Owners of the
Country on which we work, the Wurundjeri People of the
Kulin Nation and the Gadigal People of the Eora Nation, and
recognises their continuing connection to the land, waters and
culture. We pay our respects to their Elders past and present.

For all relevant publications, Hardie Grant Explore
commissions a First Nations consultant to review relevant
content and provide feedback to ensure suitable language
and information is included in the final book. Hardie
Grant Explore also includes traditional place names and
acknowledges Traditional Owners, where possible, in both
the text and mapping for their publications.

This Old Van: Plan, renovate and style your own vintage caravan
ISBN 9781741178043

10 9 8 7 6 5 4 3 2 1

Publisher Melissa Kayser
Project editor Megan Cuthbert
Editor Helena Holmgren
Editorial assistance Jenny Varghese and Lucia Morris
Proofreader Penny Mansley
Design Muse Muse
Illustrations Astred Hicks, Design Cherry
Typesetting Hannah Schubert
Index Helena Holmgren
Production coordinator Simone Wall

Colour reproduction by Hannah Schubert
and Splitting Image Colour Studio

Printed and bound in China by
LEO Paper Products LTD.

FSC
www.fsc.org
MIX
Paper from
responsible sources
FSC® C020056

The paper this book is printed on is certified
against the Forest Stewardship Council®
Standards and other sources. FSC® promotes
environmentally responsible, socially beneficial
and economically viable management of the
world's forests.